D0365915

Praying with Moses

Other titles in the Praying with the Bible Series
by Eugene H. Peterson:

Praying with Jesus
Praying with the Psalms
Praying with the Early Christians

Other titles by Eugene H. Peterson:

Answering God
Reversed Thunder

PRAYING
WITH MOSES

A Year of Daily Prayers
and Reflections
on the Words and Actions
of Moses

EUGENE H. PETERSON

HarperSanFrancisco
A Division of HarperCollinsPublishers

PRAYING WITH MOSES. *A Year of Daily Prayers and Reflections on the Words
and Actions of Moses.* Copyright © 1994 by Eugene H. Peterson. All
rights reserved. Printed in the United States of America. No part
of this book may be used or reproduced in any manner whatso-
ever without written permission except in the case of brief
quotations embodied in critical articles and reviews. For information address HarperCollins Publishers, 10 East 53rd Street,
New York, NY 10022.

FIRST EDITION

Library of Congress Cataloging-in-Publication Data
Peterson, Eugene H.
    Praying with Moses : a year of daily prayers and
reflections on the words and actions of Moses /
Eugene H. Peterson.—1st ed.
        p.   cm.
    Includes index.
    ISBN 0-06-066518-1
    1. Moses (Biblical leader)—Prayer-books and devotions—
English.   2. Devotional calendars.   3. Spiritual life—
Christianity   I. Title.
BS580.M6P47   1994
242'.2—dc20   93-45696
                                                        CIP

94 95 96 97 98 99 ❖ BANVA 9 8 7 6 5 4 3 2 1

For
Pastor Colleagues in Study and Prayer
across three decades

John H. Houdeshel
William J. Netting, Jr.
Richard W. Shreffler

Praying with Moses:
Introduction

IT IS IMPOSSIBLE to exaggerate the life-shaping, character-forming power of the words written in the first five books of the Bible. For three thousand years they have served as the foundational text for Israel and Church. Millions of men and women have pored over these words, absorbing the meanings, reflecting on the implications, letting the rhythms and sounds of the sentences work into their souls.

And more often than not the reading has turned into praying. Praying, because in the process of being read these words become personal and seem to require a personal answer.

It is widely believed that God's Holy Spirit inspired the writing of Holy Scripture. It is also widely experienced that the reading of scripture is similarly inspired, the same Holy Spirit being present and active in the current reading as in the original writing. When that happens, when "reading the Bible" becomes "praying the Bible," the text moves from our heads into our hearts, where it gives shape and energy for living, not just ideas for thinking. Such reading/praying typically brings much delight. St. Ephrem of Edessa, a fifth-century Christian in Syria, described his experience on first opening Genesis and reading: "I read the opening of the book, and was full of joy, for its verses and lines spread out their arms to welcome me; the first [sentence] rushed out and kissed me, and led me on to the next. . . ."

It should perhaps be noted that the name Moses in *Praying with Moses* designates a deep tradition rather than a strictly defined authorship. The figure of Moses towers over the formation and development of Israel's faith and the writing of scripture—virtually everything both preceding and following his actual life falls under his shadow. More than any other single person, Moses gives historical shape and brings to human expression God's word in those formative centuries of God's self-revelation. And so the first five books of the Bible have quite inevitably been called the books of Moses.

Praying with Moses has become the normative way of entering into and participating in the revelational story that is foundational for all who live by faith.

I have spread the reading, reflecting, and praying over an entire year, but not evenly. Genesis and Exodus get the most detailed treatment. With Leviticus, the nature of the material changes and it seemed desirable to reflect on and respond to larger units. But even though the story slows down considerably and there is much space given to the ordering of rituals and regulations that are no longer normative for us, there is nothing here that is not "prayable." There are spiritual treasures to be mined from these often-avoided biblical rocks.

It is well to remember, I think, that the books of Moses are the sacred text for a centuries-deep, worldwide community, and not only for scattered individuals. Small books like this one that can be carried around privately in purse or pocket can seem to give the impression that scripture and prayer are small activities, best pursued in private ways. We will read and pray more accurately when we read and pray with others, in worship and conversation, in study and friendship. It follows that the best use that can be made of *Praying with Moses* is to invite others to join you in the praying, whether in home or workplace.

Praying with Moses

JANUARY 1

"In the Beginning"

READ Genesis 1:1

In the beginning when God created the
   heavens and the earth . . . .

Genesis 1:1

God creates. Our thoughts and acts, our breathing
and hoping take place in a world creatively set in
motion by God. We never start anything. We find
the meaning of our lives not by striking out on
our own but by responding to what God has already begun in us, creating and redeeming us.

What does this beginning mean for the way
you live your life?

PRAYER: God, you are my beginning and my end:
I deliberately set myself in your creative action so
that I can participate in the great work you are
doing in the world and in me. Create in me a
clean heart and shape your will in me. *Amen.*

"Without Form and Void"

. . . the earth was a formless void and
   darkness covered the face of the deep.

Genesis 1:2a

Chaos is the raw material for God's creativity. He
can make something of nothing. His brooding
spirit is always over and in the disorder and
emptiness, bringing forth a cosmos.

What experience do you have of void and darkness?

PRAYER: Creator Spirit, when my life disintegrates
into formlessness and emptiness, when nothing
seems to fit and nothing seems to work, I will
remember these words and submit to your hover-
ing spirit, knowing that what you did once you
will do again. *Amen.*

"Light"

READ *Genesis 1:3–5*

Then God said, "Let there be light"; and
there was light.

Genesis 1:3

The first created work is light: the precondition of
life inner and outer. We live in a light-flooded existence. God originally and continually provides
that which reveals his presence and shows his
work. He does not hide in the darkness. We do
not grope in the abyss.

Why is light important to you?

PRAYER: I thank you, O God, for the light around
me and the light within me. I see what you have
made and I praise you. I see the way in which to
walk and I obey you. I see your purposes in motion and I believe you. *Amen.*

JANUARY 4

"Heaven"

READ Genesis 1:6–8

So God made the dome and separated the
waters that were under the dome from
the waters that were above the dome.
And it was so.

Genesis 1:7

Heaven is the foundational structure of creation. It
is not what we wait for in the future; it is the
firmly hammered-out base for cosmic existence.

Does the use of "heaven" here differ from your
normal use of the word?

PRAYER: God, put my feet on the firm ground of
your original creation—of heaven! Heaven not
only in the far-off skies, but heaven beneath my
feet! I want to live my life based not on what I see
and feel, but on what you provide and create.
Amen.

JANUARY 5

"Earth"

READ Genesis 1:9–13

> Then God said, "Let the earth put forth
> vegetation: plants yielding seed, and
> fruit trees of every kind on earth that
> bear fruit with the seed in it." And it
> was so.
>
> Genesis 1:11

In the midst of the heavens, earth and sea and vegetation are formed as a setting for history and faith. However much pain and discomfort and unruliness we experience here, we are aware that this place we are given to live in is planned and shaped by our wise God who pronounced it good.

Do you find fault with what God has made good?

PRAYER: In my grumbles, God, I miss the grandeur: I stub my toe on a rock and I miss the marvel of rocks. I shiver in the rain and forget the wonder of weather. I scratch my hand on a thorn and fail to smell the rose. Train me to leap and praise and dance in this incredible creation. *Amen.*

"Lights"

READ Genesis 1:14–19

God made the two great lights—the greater
light to rule the day and the lesser light
to rule the night—and the stars.

Genesis 1:16

Sun, moon, and stars are presented as God's means
for revealing time. Time involves us in both continuity and change: each day and night are different; each day and night are the same. With this
combination of freshness and stability we are neither confused nor bored.

How do the night skies affect you?

PRAYER: Eternal God, you have placed eternity in
my heart. At the same time you have placed me in
time with its hours and days and years. Show me
how to redeem the time, using each moment as a
means for loving my neighbor and praising you.
Amen.

JANUARY 7

"Every Living Creature"

READ Genesis 1:20–23

So God created the great sea monsters and
every living creature that moves, of every
kind, with which the waters swarm, and
every winged bird of every kind. And
God saw that it was good.

Genesis 1:21

The animal world is charged with marvel and
mystery; we respond at times in terror, at times in
awe. But no creature is, in principle, alien to us.
We are creatures of the same Creator. Mosquitoes
and grizzlies have their place in the interrelated
goodness that God has provided.

What part of creation do you like least?

PRAYER: God, instead of classifying everything according to my convenience, my likes and dislikes,
help me to see everything as a part of your work,
the marvelously interconnected and complemen-
tary world of goodness. *Amen.*

JANUARY 8

"In Our Image"
READ Genesis 1:24–26

Then God said, "Let us make humankind in
our image, according to our likeness. . . ."

Genesis 1:26a

Our biological kinship with lower creatures is evident, and our ecological relationship with earth
and sea and sky is demonstrable, but our personal
and spiritual origin in God is central: our deepest
and most characteristic quality is "image of God."

What does "image of God" mean to you?

PRAYER: All praise to you, Creator God! Help me
to live up to my high calling—not at the lowest
level of my biological urges but at the highest
level of my spiritual destiny. That which you created in me, bring into maturity in me, in Christ.
Amen.

JANUARY 9

"Male and Female"

So God created humankind in his image,
in the image of God he created them;
male and female he created them.

Genesis 1:27

Humanity is complete only in relationship: male
plus female equals "humankind." We cannot be
ourselves by ourselves. We are made to live in love
with each other just as we are made to live in love
with God.

Who is the most important person in your life?

PRAYER: Forgive me, Christ, when I attempt to live
to myself, selfishly and indulgently. Show me the
"other," the person who calls forth my identity
and requires my love, so that I can live my complete creation. *Amen.*

"Be Fruitful"

READ *Genesis* 1:28–30

God blessed them, and God said to them,
    "Be fruitful and multiply, and fill the
    earth and subdue it; and have dominion
    over the fish of the sea and over the
    birds of the air and over every living
    thing that moves upon the earth."

Genesis 1:28

Creation is not a museum of artifacts that we walk through and look over; it is an organism pulsating with reproductive vitalities. Nothing created is a mere "thing." We have a purpose and destiny that transcend our own immediate needs. We grow or we die.

What do you live for?

PRAYER: As you live in me, Creator Spirit, reproduce your original creative purposes in my words and actions, in the way I live and the work I do, for Jesus' sake. *Amen.*

JANUARY 11

"Very Good"

READ *Genesis* 1:31

God saw everything that he had made, and
indeed, it was very good. And there was
evening and there was morning, the
sixth day.

Genesis 1:31

Six times through the days of creation the verdict
"good" has been rendered. Now the judgment is
intensified: "very good." Whatever we may think
of this universe in which we live, the attitude of
God is not in question.

What is your attitude to the created universe
and all that is in it?

PRAYER: Help me, O God, to a deep awareness of
the goodness that permeates your creation. I complain about the people who deface your work and
I lose touch with the work itself. Restore and mature my capacity to wonder at the sheer goodness
of what is here. *Amen.*

"God Rested"

READ Genesis 2:1–4

So God blessed the seventh day and
hallowed it, because on it God rested
from all the work that he had done in
creation.

Genesis 2:3

The finishing touch is not work but rest. Being is
the conclusion to doing. The fullness of creation is
not realized in a compulsive activity, but in the
quiet contemplation of what is.

Compare this with Hebrews 4:1–10.

PRAYER: "O day of rest and gladness, O day of joy
and light, O balm of care and sadness, most beautiful, most bright; on thee the high and lowly,
through ages joined in tune, sing holy, holy,
holy, to the great God Triune" (Christopher
Wordsworth, "O Day of Rest and Goodness," in The
Hymnbook [New York: Presbyterian Church, 1955],
p. 70). Amen.

JANUARY 13

"Eden"

READ *Genesis 2:4–9*

And the LORD God planted a garden in
Eden, in the east; and there he put the
man whom he had formed.

Genesis 2:8

The creation story is intensified: Eden is the setting in which we see relationships established and
developed. Human life does not take up the most
space in creation, but it is at the center of the Creator's attention.

Note the verbs used to describe what God did.

PRAYER: Gracious God, as you speak to me in acceptance, I find that I am not just one more item
in a vast inventory but centered in your attentive
purposes. *Amen.*

JANUARY 14

"Four Rivers"

READ Genesis 2:10–14

> A river flows out of Eden to water the
> garden, and from there it divides and
> becomes four branches.
>
> Genesis 2:10

The story is focused, but it is also comprehensive. That which takes place in Eden proceeds through the four compass points to nourish the entire world. Life in Eden issues into life everywhere. The Creator is lavish, extending his largess.

Where else in the Bible are rivers featured?

PRAYER: Let my life, and all that you do in my life, O God, flow out to others in every direction. I don't want to be a stagnant pool in a private garden, but flowing with "rivers of living water" (John 7:38). Amen.

"Commanded"

READ Genesis 2:15–17

> The LORD God took the man and put him
> in the garden of Eden to till it and keep
> it. And the LORD God commanded . . .
>
> *Genesis 2:15–16a*

Everything for human wholeness is provided in the garden: good work to do, good food to eat, and a good command to obey. Leaving out any one of these elements is like leaving out one side of a triangle.

How are these elements balanced in your life?

PRAYER: I thank you, dear Father, for the work I have to do today, the food I have to eat, and the commands I have to follow. You make it possible to live at my very best to your glory. *Amen.*

"A Helper Fit for Him"

READ Genesis 2:18–23

And the rib that the LORD God had taken
from the man he made into a woman
and brought her to the man.

Genesis 2:22

God does not provide a bare biological minimum
in creation but a glorious personal richness. We
are not created to be self-sufficient. We are made
for personal relationships, and until we engage in
them we are not complete.

What are your most important personal relationships?

PRAYER: I thank you, O God, not only for creating
me, but for creating others, for placing me in a
world where I can recognize and explore the
meaning of your purposes in the gift of another
human face. *Amen.*

"One Flesh"

READ Genesis 2:24–25

Therefore a man leaves his father and his
mother and clings to his wife, and they
become one flesh.

Genesis 2:24

Community comes into existence: the basic structure of our existence is not as isolated individuals,
nor is it as competitive rivals, but as partakers of
intimate and personal relationships. At our basic
best, there is nothing to hide from the other,
nothing to withhold from the other.

To what person are you most open?

PRAYER: You know, God, how difficult it is for me
to be thoroughly honest. I am full of furtive
thoughts and guilty secrets, every one a barrier to
closeness and trust and love. For a start I will confess them to you, venturing to rely on your merciful forgiveness. *Amen.*

"Subtle"

READ Genesis 3:1–5

Now the serpent was more crafty than any
    other wild animal that the LORD God
    had made.

Genesis 3:1*a*

Temptation begins with a distortion of God's
word (v. 1), develops into a denial of it (v. 4), and
ends up with an "explanation" of it (v. 5). The
woman is cunningly drawn away from an artless
trust in God's word to a self-serving interpretation
of it.

How does temptation work in your experience?

PRAYER: Keep me alert, O God, to the peril that
comes from changing a word here and there in
your Word so that it will fit my convenience or be
more acceptable to my understanding. *Amen.*

JANUARY 19

"She Took of Its Fruit"

READ Genesis 3:6–7

So when the woman saw that the tree was
good for food, and that it was a delight
to the eyes, and that the tree was to be
desired to make one wise, she took of its
fruit and ate; and she also gave some
to her husband, who was with her, and
he ate.

Genesis 3:6

Temptation presents a view of reality exclusively
in terms of our desires. Not God's will but our
pleasure dominates awareness. The result is that
we no longer live spontaneously in grace, but
with anxious self-consciousness.

Compare verse 6 with 1 John 2:16.

PRAYER: The world's propaganda, Lord, is always
telling me that ventures into sin will extend my
experience. Your word tells me the opposite, that
my experience is constricted. Preserve me from
the tempter's lies. Keep me faithful to your gracious truth. *Amen.*

"I Hid Myself"

> . . . and the man and his wife hid
> themselves from the presence of the
> LORD God among the trees of the
> garden.

Genesis 3:8b

The intimate and relaxed relation between Creator and creature is suddenly entangled in concealments and stratagems, excuses and accusations. Temptation promised a fuller life; sin delivered a diminished life.

What is the significance of their hiding?

PRAYER: I hide behind poses, God. Fearful of what you will think of me, I assume a posture of respectability. I thank you, Father, for not letting me get by with any of it, but getting through to the truth, the actual me, and dealing with my sin through Jesus Christ. *Amen.*

"Enmity"

READ Genesis 3:14–15

> "Because you have done this,
> cursed are you among all animals
> and among all wild creatures;
> upon your belly you shall go,
> and dust you shall eat
> all the days of your life."

Genesis 3:14

The curse on the serpent describes the hostility that generally prevails between wild creatures and human beings: we were created to live in harmony; in fact, we live on guard, wary of danger, distrustful and suspicious. Our relation with the animals below us as well as the God above us is thrown into disarray.

Compare this with Romans 8:20–22.

PRAYER: I realize, Almighty God, how deeply the effects of sin have entered into the entire creation. But I realize also how much more deeply your salvation is working to make all things new, for where sin abounds, grace much more abounds. *Amen.*

JANUARY 22

"Pain"

READ *Genesis* 3:16

To the woman he said,
>   "I will greatly increase your pangs in
>   childbearing;
>   in pain you shall bring forth children,
>   yet your desire shall be for your
>   husband,
>   and he shall rule over you."

Genesis 3:16

The most magnificent privilege, giving birth to a child, is associated with the most intense pain. Even in the best experiences available to us, we are reminded of sin's legacy.

What is your most painful experience?

PRAYER: God in Christ, I know that it is futile to look for a pain-free existence, to search for some level of life where I can live in ecstasy and bliss, but I do thank you for entering into the pain and making it a means of new life and redemption, through the cross of Jesus. *Amen.*

JANUARY 23

"Sweat"

READ Genesis 3:17–19

". . . cursed is the ground because of you;
in toil you shall eat of it all the days of your
   life. . . ."

Genesis 3:17b

The ground itself, once fecund and generous (Genesis 2:9), is now harsh and grudging. The original harmony between humanity and earth is broken. The soil out of which humankind was created now becomes a reminder of its eventual death. The dismal effects of sin are inescapable.

Compare this with Genesis 2:7–9.

PRAYER: Thank you, O God, that no matter what sin does, it cannot destroy the created meaning of work (Genesis 2:15). Now give me grace to survive the difficulties that sin has introduced and still work to your glory. *Amen.*

"Eve"

READ Genesis 3:20–21

The man named his wife Eve, because she
was the mother of all living.

Genesis 3:20

Despite enigmas and penalties described in the
consequences of sin, man—defiantly hopeful—
names woman: an act of faith embracing life as a
great miracle and mystery, maintained and carried
by the woman over hardship and death.

Compare this with the naming in Genesis 2:23.

PRAYER: Life prevails over death, dear God, because you will it so. And promise overrides curse.
In the teeth of hostility, pain, and toil, blessing is
conferred. Help me to pass the blessing on to the
people I meet today. *Amen.*

JANUARY 25

"He Drove Out the Man"

READ Genesis 3:22–24

Therefore the LORD God sent him forth
from the garden of Eden, to till the
ground from which he was taken.

Genesis 3:23

Expulsion from Eden is punishment but it is also
mercy. It is punishment for acting in disobedience; it is mercy because to live forever as a
flawed, rebellious creature would be hellish.

What mercy have you experienced in judgment?

PRAYER: In the midst of your judgments, great
God, there are always mercies. I submit myself to
the discipline of your judgments and await the
salvation that comes by your mercies that are
"new every morning." *Amen.*

"Sin Is Lurking at the Door"

READ Genesis 4:1–7

"If you do well, will you not be accepted?
    And if you do not do well, sin is lurking
    at the door; its desire is for you, but you
    must master it."

Genesis 4:7

Sin is pictured as a wild animal crouching at the entrance, ready to pounce on us as we leave the security of our home to go into the world. Its intent is to control us, but we are called to establish mastery over it.

What causes rivalry between brothers?

PRAYER: Help me to see each person I meet today as my brother, my sister, not as my rival. By your spirit give me mastery over the sin that divides me from others and separates me from you. *Amen.*

"Am I My Brother's Keeper?"

READ Genesis 4:8–16

Then the LORD said to Cain, "Where is
your brother Abel?" He said, "I do not
know; am I my brother's keeper?"

Genesis 4:9

We try to improve our lives by denying responsibility toward others. All the more for ourselves!
But it doesn't work. In diminishing another in
any way, large or small, we diminish ourselves—
we lose connection, lose relationship, and are
doomed to the wasteland of selfishness.

What responsibilities do you try to evade?

PRAYER: "Thy world is weary of its pain, of selfish
greed and fruitless gain, of tarnished honor,
falsely strong, and all its ancient deeds of wrong.
Almighty Father, who dost give the gift of life to
all who live, look down on all earth's sin and strife,
and lift us to a holier life" (J. H. B. Masterman,
"Lift up Our Hearts, O King of Kings," in The Hymnbook, p. 481). Amen.

"Cain Knew His Wife"

READ Genesis 4:17–22

Cain knew his wife, and she conceived and
bore Enoch; and he built a city, and
named it Enoch after his son Enoch.

Genesis 4:17

Four occupations outline developing civilization:
city building, animal husbandry, music, and met-
allurgy. But nothing is said about God in these
lives—a gross omission! People are identified by
what they do, not by who they are. This is existence without meaning, work without purpose.

How do you identify yourself?

PRAYER: I want more than a job description for my
life, Eternal God; I want a relationship with you. I
want more than a place in history; I want a home
in eternity. Shape your will in me in mercy and
grace. *Amen.*

"Lamech Seventy-Sevenfold"

"If Cain is avenged sevenfold,
truly Lamech seventy-sevenfold."

Genesis 4:24

While civilization advances (Genesis 4:17–22), relationships deteriorate. Lamech's fiercely brutal song of revenge shows that he is not satisfied with God's promise of vengeance (4:15) but defiantly takes it into his own hands. "Sin has swelled into a landslide" (Gerhard von Rad, *Genesis* [Philadelphia, PA: Westminster Press, 1959], p. 112).

Compare this with Matthew 18:22.

PRAYER: Almighty God, the earth is wanton with vengeance, but I live in a world in which forgiveness sets all wrong right. I will leave the vengeance to you and both receive and give forgiveness, as you enable me by your Spirit. *Amen.*

"Seth"

READ Genesis 4:25–26

To Seth also a son was born, and he named
him Enosh. At that time people began to
invoke the name of the LORD.

Genesis 4:26

The line of Seth is contrasted with the line of
Cain. The line of Cain ends in the ferocity of
Lamech; the line of Seth ends in a yearning for
salvation. The lines intersect, a crossroads!

What choice do you have at this crossroads?

PRAYER: Lord God, you keep introducing unexpected innovations, fresh starts, radical surprises.
The relentless cycle of sin is interrupted. I don't
have to continue the line of Cain: I can join the
line of Seth, calling upon the name of the Lord!
Amen.

JANUARY 31

"Adam"

READ *Genesis* 5:1–5

This is the list of the descendants of Adam.
When God created humankind, he made
them in the likeness of God.

Genesis 5:1

What God began, he continued. Origins develop
into continuities. The God-likeness of Adam continues in Seth, and by implication, to everyone
since.

Why is mention of Cain omitted?

PRAYER: God, my Father, I thank you for a good
beginning and for a faithful continuing. I thank
you for evidence of ancestors who lived long and
well, passing on to me the capability of existing in
your image. *Amen.*

FEBRUARY 1

"Years"

READ Genesis 5:6–20

Seth lived after the birth of Enosh eight
  hundred seven years, and had other sons
  and daughters. Thus all the days of Seth
  were nine hundred twelve years; and
  he died.

Genesis 5:7–8

As distance from creation increases, the life span
diminishes. This is often interpreted as a gradual
deterioration of an original and wonderful vitality, a deterioration caused by the accumulating effects of sin in human nature.

Compare this with Psalm 90:10.

PRAYER: I am grateful, O God, for the years you
have given me, and the years still ahead. I receive
each year as a gift, however many or few remain.
Give me strength to live each one at my best and
to your glory, through Jesus Christ. *Amen.*

FEBRUARY 2

"Enoch Walked with God"

READ Genesis 5:21–24

Enoch walked with God; then he was no
more, because God took him.

Genesis 5:24

Our beginning is in God. Our destiny is also in
God. Much of human history is a record of forgetting our origin, wandering aimlessly, and mis-
sing our destiny. Enoch's distinction is that he did
not miss it.

What one-sentence epitaph would you like for
your life?

PRAYER: "O Master, let me walk with Thee in
lowly paths of service free; tell me Thy secret;
help me bear the strain of toil, the fret of care"
(Washington Gladden, "O Master, Let Me Walk
with Thee," in *The Hymnbook*, p. 304). *Amen.*

"God Called His Name Noah"

READ Genesis 5:25–32

> . . . he named him Noah, saying, "Out of
> the ground that the LORD has cursed this
> one shall bring us relief from our work
> and from the toil of our hands."
>
> Genesis 5:29

The naming of Noah promises relief. The great work of salvation is going to spring up from the same ground that is disfigured with thorns and thistles.

Compare this with Genesis 3:17–19.

PRAYER: God of creation and salvation, as much as I am dismayed by difficulties, I am even more heartened by promises. There is no cursed place that is not marked by your promise of salvation, for which I praise you. *Amen.*

FEBRUARY 4

"Evil Continually"

READ *Genesis 6:1–7*

The LORD saw that the wickedness of
humankind was great in the earth, and
that every inclination of the thoughts of
their hearts was only evil continually.

Genesis 6:5

The human heart is saturated with evil; God's
heart is penetrated with grief. The contrast is
poignant. The exuberant verdict "very good"
(Genesis 1:31) is shadowed by this sorrowing "I
am sorry that I have made them."

What are signs of human wickedness today?

PRAYER: I deny and avoid the evidence of evil, O
Lord: I want to pretend that everything is all right.
But it is not all right. And I am not all right. Forgive me for the sorrow that I add to your heart
by self-satisfied complacency and wayward rebellion. Save me in your mercy. *Amen.*

"But Noah Found Favor"

READ Genesis 6:8–10

But Noah found favor in the sight of the LORD.

Genesis 6:8

Noah, the last member of the old age and the first of the new, was in motion in relation to God's purpose—"he walked with God." His life went in the direction that God purposed, and followed the pace (not lagging behind, not rushing ahead) at which God acted.

What else is significant about Noah?

PRAYER: There is always an exception, God. Always there is someone who braves the derision of the crowd, steps out of the lockstep march of the evil generation, and walks with you. Give me courage to walk with you. *Amen.*

"Filled with Violence"
READ Genesis 6:11–13

Now the earth was corrupt in God's sight,
and the earth was filled with violence.

Genesis 6:11

A single word describes the worldwide corruption: violence. The contemplative rest that crowned creation (Genesis 2:3) is destroyed as men and women greedily try to own and control what God has already given and rules.

How does violence touch your life?

PRAYER: God of peace, draw me into the easy-flowing, rhythmic actions of your providence. When I try to do things my own way, I am a jerky, shoving, clutching person. When I let you do things your way, I find myself serene and blessed. Amen.

"An Ark"

READ Genesis 6:14–22

"But I will establish my covenant with you;
and you shall come into the ark, you,
your sons, your wife, and your sons'
wives with you."

Genesis 6:18

God always provides a "way of escape." Judgment is necessary because of sin; however, the consequence of sin's judgment is not the elimination of life but its rescue. Salvation is first on God's agenda.

Use 1 Corinthians 10:13 to comment on this story.

PRAYER: I thank you, merciful Lord, for evidence from the past of your will and power to save. Instruct me today, exactly and in detail, what I must do to live to your glory. *Amen*

"Seven Pairs"

READ *Genesis 7:1–5*

> Take with you seven pairs of all clean
> animals, the male and its mate; and a
> pair of the animals that are not clean, the
> male and its mate; and seven pairs of the
> birds of the air also, male and female, to
> keep their kind alive on the face of all
> the earth.

Genesis 7:2–3

Often we are so human-centered that we forget the biblical *scope* of God's mercy. Although everything is touched by sin, nothing in creation is abandoned. All living creation is included in the act of salvation and preservation.

What is the force of the expression "seven pairs"?

PRAYER: God, I don't want my life of faith to be narrowed down to saving my own skin; I want to develop a sense of community with "all creatures great and small." Extend my awareness and gratitude in all directions. *Amen.*

"The Waters of the Flood"

READ Genesis 7:6–10

> Noah was six hundred years old when the
> flood of waters came on the earth.
>
> Genesis 7:6

Chaos was commanded into order in creation
(Genesis 1:2, 6–7). Now, by God's command, the
chaos returns. It is evident now that sin was not a
minor dislocation of creation, a bothersome dis-
turbance in history. Sin is catastrophic.

What are your emotional responses to the word
"flood"?

PRAYER: As I attempt, O God, to comprehend the
totality of your judgment, help me to realize that
all my life, and everything I know about life, is
deeply disturbed by sin and must be included in
your salvation. *Amen.*

FEBRUARY 10

"The Lord Shut Him In"

READ Genesis 7:11–16

And those that entered, male and female
of all flesh, went in as God had
commanded him; and the LORD shut
him in.

Genesis 7:16

God's command does not coerce, it invites. Noah
does not rebel, he obeys. Noah's obedience is followed by God's protection. The alternative to the
way of the world, which leads to destruction, is
the way of salvation, in which God takes charge of
the preservation of his people.

How do you respond to God's commands?

PRAYER: I thank you, Almighty God, for your secure protection. Relieved of anxiety for defending
myself, I am free to risk my life in faith, obeying
your commands and enjoying your salvation.
Amen.

"The Ark Floated"

READ Genesis 7:17–24

The waters swelled and increased greatly
on the earth; and the ark floated on the
face of the waters.

Genesis 7:18

Two realities often obscured through inattention
or trivialized by clichés are in focus: the enormity
of sin and the miracle of salvation. Our sins cannot be exaggerated; grace is triumphant.

Enumerate the contrasts in this passage.

PRAYER: God of judgment and grace, I submit myself to your decrees and discover the miracle of
your victorious will. Bring me through whatever
is needed to train and prepare me to live in serious and joyful faith. *Amen.*

"God Remembered Noah"

READ Genesis 8:1–5

> But God remembered Noah and all the
> wild animals and all the domestic
> animals that were with him in the ark.
>
> Genesis 8:1a

The wind that moved over the waters preparing for creation (Genesis 1:2) now moves over the waters preparing for salvation. God's spirit (wind) is never exhausted, never inert. God begins, and he begins again. As the waters of judgment recede, the mountains of salvation appear.

Where is Ararat?

PRAYER: You never give up, O God; don't let me ever give up. Let no judgment, no catastrophe, no dislocation in my life permit me to lose touch with your marvelous, persistent will to salvation, worked out in me and throughout the world. Amen.

FEBRUARY 13

"The Dove"

READ Genesis 8:6–12

Then he sent out the dove from him, to see
if the waters had subsided from the face
of the ground; but the dove found no
place to set its foot, and it returned to
him to the ark, for the waters were still
on the face of the whole earth. So he put
out his hand and took it and brought it
into the ark with him.

Genesis 8:8–9

Is there in the dove's flight over the angry waters
of judgment a reminiscence of the Spirit's hover-
ing over the waters of chaos (Genesis 1:2)? At any
rate, dove and Spirit are forever associated in our
minds with creative beginnings.

Where are other important references to the
dove?

PRAYER: Spirit of God, signal new life in me. Out
of the wasteland of sin, the leftover debris of
judgment, show me evidence of your salvation.
Amen.

"Go Out of the Ark"

READ *Genesis 8:13–22*

Then God said to Noah, "Go out of the
ark, you and your wife, and your sons
and your sons' wives with you."

Genesis 8:15–16

Tumbling out of the ark, Noah, his family, and all
animals become God's obedient life-bringers. The
ark was not a permanent hideout, but a tempo-
rary means of rescue—salvation expands outward,
populating and blessing the earth with new life.

Where do you feel safest?

PRAYER: I feel so safe and get so comfortable in the
place of salvation, Lord, that I am reluctant to
brave the world's weather. But you command an
exit: "go out." Give me daily courage and hope to
obey. *Amen.*

"Lifeblood"

READ Genesis 9:1–7

"For your own lifeblood I will surely
    require a reckoning: from every animal I
    will require it and from human beings,
    each one for the blood of another, I will
    require a reckoning for human life."

Genesis 9:5

Life is abundant, but it is not cheap. After the flood the preciousness of life is more evident than ever. What God has created and preserved requires vigilant protection and reverent respect.

Why do some people hold human life in low esteem?

PRAYER: So many things, God, compete with life for prominence: ideas, objects, causes. Do not let me be tricked or deceived into thinking that anything has more value than a single human life, made in your image, redeemed by Christ's blood. Amen.

FEBRUARY 16

"Never Again"

READ Genesis 9:8–17

"I have set my bow in the clouds, and it
shall be a sign of the covenant between
me and the earth."

Genesis 9:13

The bow is characteristically a weapon, but it is now at rest. God is not in pursuit of an enemy; he is in covenant with his people. The Creator has won his victory over chaos. Confident of eventual peace, he promises never again to be at war with his creation.

What do you think of when you see a rainbow?

PRAYER: "Sometimes a light surprises the Christian while he sings; it is the Lord, who rises with healing in His wings: when comforts are declining, He grants the soul again a season of clear shining, to cheer it after rain" (William Cowper, "Sometimes a Light Surprises," in *The Hymnbook*, p. 418). *Amen.*

"Sons of Noah"

These three were the sons of Noah; and
from these the whole earth was peopled.

Genesis 9:19

The story expands. Up until now it has been a
story of individuals; now it is a story of peoples
and nations. The biblical story is not restricted to
the personal and individual; it spreads out to the
political and the global. God so loved the world.

What nation other than your own do you know
best about?

PRAYER: God of the nations, I know that you love
and are at work in all peoples on every continent.
But I don't act like it: I somehow think you have
special liking for us and are, deep down, on our
side. Train me to think extravagantly of your
grace. Amen.

"Cursed Be Canaan"

READ Genesis 9:20–29

. . . he said,
  "Cursed be Canaan;
  lowest of slaves shall he be to his brothers."

Genesis 9:25

Two sons were obedient and were blessed; one son was disobedient and was cursed. The conflict between Israel, with its respect for the mysteries and morality of life, and Canaan, with its notoriously disordered sexual practices and manipulative religion, is traced to this event.

What other conflicts between brothers do you remember?

PRAYER: You command me to honor my father and my mother, O God: involve me in a life of respect. It is easy to find fault with my ancestors and expose their errors; it is always better to be grateful for their heritage and celebrate their life of faith. Amen.

"The Nations Spread Abroad"

READ Genesis 10:1–32

> These are the families of Noah's sons,
> according to their genealogies, in their
> nations; and from these the nations
> spread abroad on the earth after the
> flood.
>
> Genesis 10:32

Though this is hardly the most "inspirational" chapter in Genesis, it is necessary to keep us in touch with a basic but often-denied reality—the essential kinship of everyone and every nation on earth. Beneath all differences, whether racial or political, there is a deep, underlying unity that is God-given.

Compare this with Acts 17:26–28.

PRAYER: "God bless the men and women who serve Him overseas; God raise up more to help them to set the nations free, till all the distant people in every foreign place shall understand His Kingdom and come into His grace" (Percy Dearmer, "Remember All the People," in The Hymnbook, p. 495). Amen.

"Make a Name"

READ Genesis 11:1–4

> Then they said, "Come, let us build
> ourselves a city, and a tower with its top
> in the heavens, and let us make a name
> for ourselves; otherwise we shall be
> scattered abroad upon the face of the
> whole earth."

Genesis 11:4

People are already one in creation. From that integrated, harmonious unity, peace flows across the earth. This tower-building was an attempt to supplant the original unity with an imposed, manufactured unity—to take over God's rule and be worshiped instead of worshiping.

How do you imagine the tower to have looked?

PRAYER: Your name be exalted, Almighty God, not mine. Holy be your name, not mine. Your name be praised; your name be proclaimed; in Jesus' name. Amen.

"Babel"

READ Genesis 11:5–9

And the LORD said, "Look, they are one
people, and they have all one language;
and this is only the beginning of what
they will do; nothing that they propose
to do will now be impossible for them."

Genesis 11:6

Why is there so much talk and so little understanding? Why does the great gift of language so
often end up in jargon? When language is used to
manipulate people instead of to adore God, to get
our own way instead of being in communication
with God's way, it falls into confusion.

Contrast this with Acts 2:6.

PRAYER: I talk too much and don't listen enough,
dear God. In these moments of prayer I retreat
from the noisy world, and enter the silence so that
I can learn to speak again—in praise, in truth, in
love. *Amen.*

"The Descendants of Shem"

READ Genesis 11:10–26

These are the descendants of Shem. When
Shem was one hundred years old, he
became the father of Arpachshad two
years after the flood; and Shem lived
after the birth of Arpachshad five
hundred years, and had other sons and
daughters.

Genesis 11:10–11

This list is in parallel with chapter 10: that list
widens out to include all the families of the earth;
this list narrows down to focus on Abram, the
father of the faithful. In the first, there is compre-
hension; in this one, concentration. The wide-
screen panorama gives way to a close-up of what
God is doing with one people.

Who are important ancestors in your past?

PRAYER: I don't recognize most of these names,
Lord, but I do see that they are names and realize
that what is significant in the past is not a list of
ideas but a succession of persons in whom you
are working out your purposes. Continue that
work in me. *Amen.*

"Sarai Was Barren"

READ Genesis 11:27–30

Now Sarai was barren; she had no child.

Genesis 11:30

The command at the creation and again at the new creation (Genesis 1:28 and 9:1) was "Be fruitful and multiply." But how? Sarai is barren. There is an abyss between what God intends and what, in fact, is humanly possible. If there is going to be a continuation of this story, it will have to be a story about what God does, not what men and women do.

What is "impossible" in your life?

PRAYER: Lord God, when I am faced with my inadequacy, I despair. Then I realize that that is the precondition for your best work: that your grace is sufficient for me, that your strength is made perfect in my weakness. *Amen.*

"Go"

READ *Genesis 12:1–3*

Now the LORD said to Abram, "Go from
your country and your kindred and your
father's house to the land that I will
show you."

Genesis 12:1

God's terse command signals a new beginning.
Everything must be left behind in this venture
into a life of faith. The triple renunciation (country, kindred, house) releases Abram for free obedience. Five promises are made to Abram as he is
commanded out of a life of emptiness into a life
of fullness. The blessing that is initiated in Abram
does not end with him—this is a beginning that
will have consequences for all humankind.

Compare this with Jesus' words in Mark 8:35.

PRAYER: Command me, O God, into the future
you have for me. Release me from all attachments
that prevent obedience. Give me ears to hear and
a will to respond to your promises. Everywhere I
look, every direction in which I go, I discover the
fullness of life prepared by your gracious purposes, through Jesus Christ my Lord. *Amen.*

FEBRUARY 25

"So Abram Went"

READ Genesis 12:4–6

> So Abram went, as the LORD had told him;
> and Lot went with him. Abram was
> seventy-five years old when he departed
> from Haran.
>
> Genesis 12:4

Abram doesn't speak, he goes. He doesn't discuss, he obeys. He journeys in "a majestic simplicity" (Gerhard von Rad, *Genesis*, p. 161) in which all security is abandoned and the uncertainties of the journey are engaged.

Compare this with Hebrews 11:8–12.

PRAYER: Your call, God, puts me in motion. Show me how to find the meaning of my life, not in holding on but in letting go, not in trying to carve out a niche for myself but by taking the journey that you command. *Amen.*

"He Built There an Altar"

READ Genesis 12:7–9

Then the LORD appeared to Abram, and
said, "To your offspring I will give this
land." So he built there an altar to the
LORD, who had appeared to him.

Genesis 12:7

The pilgrimage of faith does not take place in a
vacuum. The Canaanites in the land offered a
stable and successful alternative to faith. But
rather than accommodating himself to the culture
of the Canaanites, Abram built altars at each stopping place, orienting himself afresh to the word
of God.

Use Acts 4:12 to comment on this passage.

PRAYER: In the midst of other voices that give advice and make claims, I will make sure there is
space in my life to attend exclusively to you, O
God. I call on your name in praise for your goodness, and in petition for your help, through Jesus
Christ. Amen.

"Down to Egypt"

READ Genesis 12:10–16

> Now there was a famine in the land. So
> Abram went down to Egypt to reside
> there as an alien, for the famine was
> severe in the land.
>
> Genesis 12:10

Abram, full of faith when he responded to God's call, is now full of anxiety, a man of unfaith, willing to risk his wife to save his own life. But God's purpose encompasses both Abram's faith and his anxiety. Abram did not continue faithful; God did continue faithful.

What are you most anxious about these days?

PRAYER: Faithful God, keep me faithful. I waver and I retreat. Dangers and threats obscure the promises you make. But though I forget you, you do not forget me. Thank you for your unsleeping mercy. *Amen.*

"Be Gone"

READ Genesis 12:17–20

"Why did you say, 'She is my sister,' so that
I took her for my wife? Now then, here
is your wife, take her, and be gone."

Genesis 12:19

There is an Egyptian side to this story: it is dangerous to deal with people of faith. Worldly forces cannot with impunity work their will on God's people, even when those people are faithless. No one is a mere human being—it is the image and purpose of God that they are dealing with, whether they are aware of it or not.

Compare Abraham and Pharaoh.

PRAYER: God of all peoples and nations, stretch my imagination to see you working in all persons and all events, not only in those whom I name religious, not only in the people I recognize as believers. *Amen.*

"Very Rich"

READ Genesis 13:1–7

So Abram went up from Egypt, he and his
wife, and all that he had, and Lot with
him, into the Negeb.

Genesis 13:1

Here is Abram in a very different setting: he has
just been in Egypt full of anxiety, barely surviving;
now he is abundantly rich, faced with the prob-
lem of too much. Poverty provides one set of
problems, wealth another. Abraham faced both.

How does the place Bethel function in this
story?

PRAYER: Whether I have much or little, O God,
lead me into the faith that seeks your kingdom
first. Let me not suppose that poverty is a curse or
wealth a blessing, but find in whatever state I am
contentment in pursuing your will. *Amen.*

"The Whole Land"

READ Genesis 13:8–13

Then Abram said to Lot, "Let there be no
strife between you and me, and between
your herders and my herders; for we are
kindred."

Genesis 13:8

Abundance does not characteristically make people generous; more often it makes us miserly,
greedy for more. But Abram was generous. Nurturing relationships ("we are kindred") was far more
important to him than maintaining possessions.

Do you ever sacrifice people for things?

PRAYER: Lord God, as you have given, so help me
to give. I don't want to be a person who grasps
and clings, but one who releases and shares, even
as you have in Jesus Christ. *Amen.*

"Lift Up Your Eyes"

READ Genesis 13:14–18

". . . for all the land that you see I will give
to you and to your offspring forever."

Genesis 13:15

When Abram gave the best of the land to Lot, he
was not diminished but augmented; he had not
less but more. God's covenant blessing is reaf-
firmed in all directions and into the future. The
eyes of faith see farther and deeper than the eyes
of ambition.

Compare this with Genesis 12:1–3.

PRAYER: Dear God, my nearsightedness prevents
me from seeing the vast land of promises and
blessing stretching out across the horizon. Heal
my vision as I lift up my eyes. *Amen.*

"War"

.. these kings made war. . . .

Genesis 14:2a

The personal story of Abram and the life of faith is interrupted with this report on an international war. Faith is never allowed to develop quietly in out-of-the-way corners in the desert; it must deal not only with the one God but with the nine kings—human violence and power struggles.

What current events demand your attention at this time?

PRAYER: Almighty God, as you train me to live by faith, show me how to face and deal with outer events as well as inward feelings, the violence in the world as well as dispositions of the spirit. Amen.

"I Will Take Nothing"

READ Genesis 14:13–24

> "I will take nothing but what the young
> men have eaten, and the share of the
> men who went with me—Aner, Eshcol,
> and Mamre. Let them take their share."

Genesis 14:24

Abram refuses to act like a typical victorious king, enriching himself with the spoils of battle. He gives! He uses the occasion of triumph to affirm his faith and witness to his God. The shadowy figure of Melchizedek corroborates this affirmation and witness.

Review and compare this with Hebrews 5:6–10.

PRAYER: I am far more likely to drift from you, O God, when I am prosperous than when I am needy. Abram shows me the way to trust you in the euphoria of victory as well as call on you in the anguish of need. I want my praises to be as vigorous as my petitions. *Amen.*

MARCH 6

"I Continue Childless"

READ Genesis 15:1–6

He brought him outside and said, "Look
toward heaven and count the stars, if you
are able to count them." Then he said to
him, "So shall your descendants be."

Genesis 15:5

Time passes. Promises are repeated. History develops. But there is no child. A disturbing question
develops within Abram. How long is it possible to
live by faith without some confirmation in everyday reality? God does not begin by answering
Abram's question; he shifts Abram's attention
from his household to God's heavens.

What promise is not fulfilled in your life?

PRAYER: I too, Lord, regularly look in the wrong
direction: I examine my own resources; I assess
the possibilities around me; I don't find much. I
will look beyond, upward, God-ward and attend
to the new worlds that come into being at your
command. *Amen.*

"How Am I to Know?"

READ Genesis 15:7–11

> But he said, "O LORD God, how am I to
> know that I shall possess it?"
>
> Genesis 15:8

Faith does not exclude questions. Abram believed but he continued to ask questions. The father of all who believe is also the father of those who ask questions. And God does not ignore or reject our questions. There are ways of dealing with our questions that do not dilute faith.

What are some of your questions?

PRAYER: Instead of suppressing what I am curious about and avoiding the hard questions that get between me and you, O God, teach me how to submit them to your treatment. I want to bring my doubting questions as well as my faithful obedience into your presence. Amen.

MARCH 8

"A Dread and Great Darkness"

READ Genesis 15:12–21

On that day the LORD made a covenant with
Abram, saying, "To your descendants I
give this land, from the river of Egypt to
the great river, the river Euphrates. . . ."

Genesis 15:18

A commitment to a life of faith is not a way to get
things done in a hurry: mature believers wait a
lot. Abram is led into the corridors of history
where much is fearsome and dark; he learns that
the promises are fulfilled through the centuries,
and not without much suffering. The details of
this ritual are obscure, but the point is clear: the
unconscious Abram and the unseen God are connected at a deeper level than seeing—they are in
covenant, bound together: human faith and faithful God.

How does your impatience interfere with your
faith?

PRAYER: I am so self-centered in my faith, dear
God. I think exclusively about what I will get out
of it, and when. Train me in God-centeredness;
put me in touch with the large, generational
rhythms of your promise-keeping. *Amen.*

"The Voice of Sarai"

READ Genesis 16:1–2

. . . and Sarai said to Abram, "You see that
the LORD has prevented me from bearing
children; go in to my slave-girl; it may
be that I shall obtain children by her."
And Abram listened to the voice of Sarai.

Genesis 16:2

The deep faith that developed through Abram's
questions is now undermined from another direction: the attempt of Sarai to be helpful. Faith
has as much to fear from good intentions as from
evil opposition. The voice of Sarai, no matter how
sincere, is not the voice of God.

Whose good intentions have made life difficult
for you?

PRAYER: I know that many of the people around
me, God, are only trying to help me in the way of
faith. But they want to do it in their way, not
yours. Help me to discriminate between their
good intentions and their bad advice. *Amen.*

MARCH 10

"Sarai Dealt Harshly"

READ Genesis 16:3–6

Then Sarai dealt harshly with her, and she
ran away from her.

Genesis 16:6b

The plan worked but the results were unhappy.
That is the usual pattern in these things: we get
what we wanted and then find out that we don't
like what we wanted.

What plans have backfired on you?

PRAYER: One minute, O God, I am selflessly attempting to get your will done in those around
me; the next minute I am angry and fretful because I don't like the way I am treated in the
consequences. Forgive me for my emotional pet-
tiness, but more than that, teach me to live by a
deeper faith. *Amen.*

"The Angel of the Lord Found Her"

READ Genesis 16:7–16

The angel of the LORD also said to her, "I
   will so greatly multiply your offspring
   that they cannot be counted for
   multitude."

Genesis 16:10

The fleeing Hagar is found by the ministering
angel. Sarai's jealous anger is counteracted by the
angel's generous comfort. But in the midst of the
comfort there is a prophecy of conflict. Sarai's unfaith is going to wreak havoc through the centuries.

How is Hagar important for understanding a
life of Christ?

PRAYER: I am beginning to realize, Almighty God,
that I cannot escape the consequences of other
people's sins—nor other people mine. We are
bound up in this life of covenant together. Lead us
all in mercy even as we experience judgment,
through Jesus Christ our Lord. Amen.

"Multiply"

READ *Genesis* 17:1–14

No longer shall your name be Abram, but
your name shall be Abraham; for I have
made you the ancestor of a multitude of
nations.

Genesis 17:5

The promise grows, intensifies, and expands; it
does not diminish through the waiting years. The
expansiveness is signaled in a name change: from
Abram, "father exalted," to Abraham, "father of a
multitude."

Do you ever reduce God's promises?

PRAYER: Father Almighty, I don't want to reduce
your promise to fit my diminishing expectations;
instead, help me to respond believingly to the
developing ramifications of what you speak,
through my Lord and Savior Jesus Christ. *Amen.*

"Fell on His Face and Laughed"
READ *Genesis 17:15–17*

Then Abraham fell on his face and laughed,
and said to himself, "Can a child be
born to a man who is a hundred years
old? Can Sarah, who is ninety years old,
bear a child?"

Genesis 17:17

Abraham's laughter had no gaiety in it; it was sheer involuntary disbelief. In his disbelief he tries to manipulate God into using what is a sure thing, Ishmael. He is, understandably, impatient with the risks and uncertainties of faith. But God will not be diverted.

What is the hardest thing for you to believe?

PRAYER: I say I believe, great God, but I don't act like it. I haven't yet absorbed the great mysteries into my inner life so that I live them spontaneously. But I want to, by your grace. *Amen.*

"That Very Day"

READ Genesis 17:18–27

That very day Abraham and his son Ishmael
were circumcised. . . .

Genesis 17:26

Abraham doubted but he did not procrastinate.
When something was commanded, he did it. His
obedience was unhesitating, and in his obedience
he acted himself into mature faith.

What command are you putting off until tomorrow?

PRAYER: Lord, you know that I like to wait until I
see how things turn out before I commit myself
unconditionally. But Abraham committed himself
unconditionally so that he would be part of the
way things turned out. Help me to do it Abraham's
way. Amen.

MARCH 15

"The Oaks of Mamre"
READ Genesis 18:1–8

> He looked up and saw three men standing
>   near him. When he saw them, he ran
>   from the tent entrance to meet them,
>   and bowed down to the ground.
>
> Genesis 18:2

Abraham, with no indication that his visitors are
"the Lord," is yet energetically hospitable. The appearance of travelers is no intrusion but presents
him with the honor to act as host. Thus Abraham's ordinary, everyday character is the material
condition in which extraordinary revelation takes
place.

Compare this with Hebrews 13:2.

PRAYER: Almighty God, how many times do I miss
meeting you because I am contemptuous or indif-
ferent to the people around me, or resentful of in-
terruptions? Give me the gift of hospitality and
train me in its manners. *Amen.*

"So Sarah Laughed"

READ Genesis 18:9–15

So Sarah laughed to herself, saying, "After I
have grown old, and my husband is old,
shall I have pleasure?"

Genesis 18:12

Disbelief erupts in laughter at the absurdity of
promise in a life of barrenness. For by this time
Sarah has come to terms with her childless state.
But God does not permit us to "come to terms"
with an unfulfilled life. The "impossible" jars us
out of the rut of unbelief.

Would you have laughed?

PRAYER: Your promises are not jokes to be laughed
at, O God, but maps that chart a faith walk. Still,
your promises regularly outdistance my capacity
to hope and believe. Enlarge my heart to take in
your blessings. Amen.

"The Outcry Against Sodom"

READ Genesis 18:16–21

Then the LORD said, "How great is the
outcry against Sodom and Gomorrah
and how very grave their sin!"

Genesis 18:20

Willful, self-indulgent, godless living finally results in a general outrage. Humanity will not forever stand for a violation of its basic being.
Judgment is not arbitrarily imposed from above;
it rises out of violated, outraged humanity.

What present conditions in the world impel
you to protest?

PRAYER: I join my voice, Almighty God, to all
those who are passionate in protest against the arrogantly cruel, the defiantly evil. We petition your
judgment against all who hurt people and who
deface creation, for Jesus' sake. Amen.

"Suppose Ten Are Found There"

READ Genesis 18:22–33

Then he said, "Oh do not let the Lord be
angry if I speak just once more. Suppose
ten are found there." He answered, "For
the sake of ten I will not destroy it."

Genesis 18:32

Judgment is not the blind bulldozing of polluted
society. It is a careful, discriminating dealing with
what is wrong. Abraham's compassionate intercession and God's merciful attentiveness show us
that there is nothing arbitrary or vengeful in the
operations of the divine judgment.

Why is intercession important?

PRAYER: Lord, in my concern for justice, never let
my anger over wickedness overbalance my passion for mercy. I want my prayer life, like Abraham's, to be saturated with intercession, not
imprecation. In the name of Jesus Christ our Lord.
Amen.

"Up, Get out of This Place"

READ Genesis 19:1–14

So Lot went out and said to his sons-in-law,
who were to marry his daughters, "Up,
get out of this place; for the LORD is
about to destroy the city."

Genesis 19:14a

The gracious hospitality at the oaks of Mamre (Genesis 18:1–8) is contrasted with this violated hospitality in Sodom. Every person is precious and must be treated with gentle dignity; the violent indignities associated with this city make it intolerable for human habitation.

Observe other contrasts between Genesis 18:1–8 and this passage.

PRAYER: Don't let me, Lord, like Lot, get so used to what is going on all around me that I don't even notice the enormity of the evil. I want to be ardent in pursuit of justice, not complacent in acquiescence to evil. *Amen.*

"He Lingered"

READ *Genesis 19:15–28*

> But he lingered; so the men seized him and his wife and his two daughters by the hand, the LORD being merciful to him, and they brought him out and left him outside the city.

Genesis 19:16

Lot's reluctance to be saved and the nostalgia of Lot's wife for her past life are legendary. They are contrasted with the utter devastation that judgment effects on all sin and all the products of sin. We cannot keep a foot in both worlds, one in the city of sin, one in the country of faith.

Does the text in Revelation 3:15–21 apply to Lot?

PRAYER: Work the grace of repentance, O God, thoroughly and deeply in my life, separating me absolutely from everything that ties us to "the world, the flesh, and the devil," so that I can experience the freedom of faith through Jesus Christ. *Amen.*

"God Destroyed the Cities"

READ *Genesis 19:29–38*

So it was that, when God destroyed the
cities of the Plain, God remembered
Abraham, and sent Lot out of the midst
of the overthrow, when he overthrew
the cities in which Lot had settled.

Genesis 19:29

God is the Lord of beginnings and endings. Out of
each ending a new beginning is launched. The
story of Lot and his descendants, while not at the
center of the biblical story of salvation, serves as a
witness that all (even Moabites and Ammonites!)
owe their existence to grace.

What do you know about Moab and Ammon?

PRAYER: I am learning, Eternal God, that there is
no detail in the human story that does not begin
in the faith story. Although sin interferes and mars
in many ways, the story line is always there—the
grace of our Lord Jesus Christ! *Amen.*

"He Sojourned in Gerar"

READ Genesis 20:1–7

Abraham said of his wife Sarah, "She is my
sister." And King Abimelech of Gerar
sent and took Sarah.

Genesis 20:2

Abraham, the "knight of faith," is again flat on his
face, faithless. He not only sins, he repeats his
sins, for he had used Sarah this way before. In
contrast, the pagan Abimelech acts with "integrity."
Compare this with Genesis 12:10–13.

PRAYER: Faithful God, I throw myself on your
mercy. I don't learn very fast, I repeat old sins. My
pride and my fears keep getting in the way of your
promises. Forgive me. Put me in the way of faith
again by your grace. Amen.

"God Healed Abimelech"

READ Genesis 20:8–18

Then Abraham prayed to God; and God
healed Abimelech, and also healed his
wife and female slaves so that they bore
children.

Genesis 20:17

The morally superior Abimelech is dependent on
the flawed and faithless Abraham. Clearly, Abraham's preeminence is not a result of his virtue but
comes from God's promises. God's grace overrules the infamy of Abraham and the infirmity of
Abimelech.

What other contrasts are there between Abraham and Abimelech?

PRAYER: Your incredible grace, great God, works
in the midst of sin and ignorance, arrogance and
willfulness. And so I live in continuing hope that
you will finally lead my wandering feet into the
path of discipleship. Amen.

"Sarah Conceived"

READ Genesis 21:1–7

Sarah conceived and bore Abraham a son
in his old age, at the time of which God
had spoken to him

Genesis 21:2

Everything leads up to this text; everything hangs
on it. Everything prepares for this, but nothing
explains it. God does it. Biology and theology
converge. The life of faith integrates God's word
and fleshly existence. Abraham and Sarah brought
only their helplessness, their tired, aged reality to
this event; God brought creation and resurrection.
The promise does not complete what we begin; it
is resurrection in the midst of our dead and deso-
late emptiness. Laughter, not logic, is the characteristic mode of witness.

How is this birth like Jesus' birth?

PRAYER: I live by promise, O God: let me never
forget that. Help me to keep your promises clear
and shining, and my responses alert and courageous, so that nothing will be impossible for you
in my life. *Amen.*

MARCH 25

"Cast out This Slave Woman"

READ Genesis 21:8–14

> So she said to Abraham, "Cast out this slave
> woman with her son; for the son of this
> slave woman shall not inherit along with
> my son Isaac."
>
> Genesis 21:10

The celebrated birth of Isaac is linked with the anguished life of Ishmael. Sarah laughs over Isaac; she is provoked to jealousy over Ishmael. But Abraham refuses to reject him, and takes care to preserve him.

Note how Paul uses this story in Galatians 4:30.

PRAYER: I like neat, black-and-white solutions to life, Lord, but the existence you invite me into is ambiguous: there is the miracle of Isaac, but there is also the fact of Ishmael. Like Sarah I would like to banish what doesn't fit into my scheme; but your scheme is larger than mine. Show me how to live in your larger providence. *Amen.*

MARCH 26

"What Troubles You, Hagar?"

> And God heard the voice of the boy; and
> the angel of God called to Hagar from
> heaven, and said to her, "What troubles
> you, Hagar? Do not be afraid; for God has
> heard the voice of the boy where he is."
>
> Genesis 21:17

Hagar and Ishmael are not the center of the story,
but we are made to understand that God's mercy
is as diligent in their lives as in any others. There
are no fringe people in the story of faith. Grace is
everywhere.

What is the significance of Ishmael in the faith
story?

PRAYER: Gracious and merciful Christ, train me in
alertness and compassion so that I will hear the
cry of the destitute and see the tears of the dis-
traught and be merciful in your strong and compassionate name. *Amen.*

"God Is with You"

READ Genesis 21:22–34

> At that time Abimelech, with Phicol
> the commander of his army, said to
> Abraham, "God is with you in all that
> you do. . . ."
>
> Genesis 21:22

The non-Israelite Abimelech recognizes God's purposes being worked out in the Israelite Abraham. Abraham is already giving evidence of what was promised earlier, that in him "all the families of the earth shall be blessed" (Genesis 12:3).

Whose life is evidence to you of God's blessing?

PRAYER: God of blessing, use my life as a witness that you are at work for good and not for ill, that you intend salvation. I pray that nothing I say or do today may contradict what you are doing in the people I meet. *Amen.*

"God Tested Abraham"

READ Genesis 22:1–6

After these things God tested Abraham.
He said to him, "Abraham!" And he said,
"Here I am."

Genesis 22:1

Does the God who promises also test? Does the God who blesses with miraculous new life also command the giving up of that life? We have, it seems, no easy-to-understand God. There is more to the life of faith than we bargained for. There are difficulties here "past finding out."

What does "testing" mean to you?

PRAYER: Almighty God, just when I think I have your ways figured out, I find there is more to them than I thought, and I am plunged into mystery again—stretched beyond my comfortable routines into acts that require no less than everything. Help my unbelief. *Amen.*

"Walked on Together"

READ Genesis 22:7–8

Abraham said, "God himself will provide
the lamb for a burnt offering, my son."
So the two of them walked on together.

Genesis 22:8

The father and the son walk together in faith. The
son, naively innocent, walks confidently in his father's assurance. The father, full of foreboding,
walks in the conviction of a long obedience. In
the life of faith, feelings fluctuate and differ, but
obedience puts us on the way.

Do you ever confuse feelings with faith?

PRAYER: Faithful God, help me to treat my feelings
as what they are—just feelings. Lead me in the
path of obedience and shape a life of faithfulness
in me that is based on your word, not my emotions. *Amen.*

"Bound Isaac His Son"

READ Genesis 22:9–12

When they came to the place that God had
   shown him, Abraham built an altar there
   and laid the wood in order. He bound
   his son Isaac, and laid him on the altar,
   on top of the wood.

Genesis 22:9

We want a God who comforts but does not stretch
us. We want a God who promises but does not
test us. But we will not find such a God in the
Bible: Abraham is tested to the limit; his faith
takes him to the limit.

What is the extremity in which you have been
tested?

PRAYER: God, ready me for hearing and obeying
your word in the face of the world's cynicism and
in defiance of my own self-seeking. I want your
will in every part of my life and my will crucified.
Amen.

"Abraham Looked up"

READ Genesis 22:13–14

And Abraham looked up and saw a ram,
   caught in a thicket by its horns. Abraham
   went and took the ram and offered it up
   as a burnt offering instead of his son.

Genesis 22:13

The God who tests is identical with the God who provides. The entire episode of testing is set in the context of God's care and provision. He sees everything we need and leads us to the place where we also see what he gives for our salvation.

How many times is "provide" used?

PRAYER: God, my sense of need is so determined by anxiety that I grab at whatever is right before me and so miss the gracious provisions that are out of my immediate sight. Slow me down long enough to become aware of the grand sweep of your providence in my life, through Christ my Lord. Amen.

APRIL 1

"I Will Indeed Bless You"

READ Genesis 22:15–19

". . . I will indeed bless you, and I will
make your offspring as numerous as the
stars of heaven and as the sand that is on
the seashore."

Genesis 22:17a

Having traveled through the narrow defile of testing, Abraham now enters the wide expanse of blessing. The consequences of faith are characterized by abundance, overflow. Renunciation becomes plenitude.

Compare this with the first promise in Genesis 12:2–3.

PRAYER: God of blessing, receive my deep thanks for the richness and graciousness that I discover filling my days. Continue to lead me in the abundant way, and guard me from the sterile detours of sin. *Amen.*

"These Eight"

READ Genesis 22:20–24

Bethuel became the father of Rebekah.
    These eight Milcah bore to Nahor,
    Abraham's brother.

Genesis 22:23

Obscure names, while not as exciting as dramatic narratives, are just as important for understanding God's ways among us. God is working not only with the center-stage people, but also with the behind-the-scenes people who will never be the subject of a sermon.

What names do you recognize?

PRAYER: Dear God, keep me attentive to overlooked persons so that my life of faith engages in love and courtesy, in service and compassion. I don't want to know just the stories of how you work, but also the persons with whom you work. Amen.

"And Sarah Died"

READ Genesis 23:1–2

And Sarah died at Kiriath-arba (that is,
    Hebron) in the land of Canaan; and
    Abraham went in to mourn for Sarah
    and to weep for her.

Genesis 23:2

Sarah had lied for Abraham (Genesis 12:10–20), mocked the promise (18:9–15), and finally laughed the resurrection laugh (21:6). She was a full partner with Abraham in everything—the sin, the absurdity, the faith.

Where and how do you identify with Sarah?

PRAYER: Eternal God, all of life is in your hand, and all our days are lived empowered by your promises. I give you thanks for the life of Sarah and its shaping power on my life as a participant in the story of salvation. Amen.

"The Cave of Machpelah"

READ Genesis 23:3–20

So the field of Ephron in Machpelah,
    which was to the east of Mamre, the
    field with the cave that was in it and
    all the trees that were in the field,
    throughout its whole area, passed to
    Abraham as a possession in the presence
    of the Hittites, in the presence of all
    who went in at the gate of his city.

Genesis 23:17–18

Abraham was a sojourner—a pilgrim seeking a "better country" (Hebrews 11:16) than any he had come across in his extensive travels. But Sarah's death required a burial plot. A grave became the first sign of possession of the land. For people of faith still, graves mark not an end but a beginning.

What kind of associations do burial plots have for you?

PRAYER: Almighty God, as the lives of people I know and love come to an end, help me to recognize in these deaths and burials evidence of completed promises and fulfilled hope, even as I anticipate the time when "this perishable body puts on imperishability" (1 Corinthians 15:54). Amen.

"Take a Wife for My Son"

". . . he will send his angel before you, and
you shall take a wife for my son from
there."

Genesis 24:7b

Isaac needs a wife so that the fulfilling of the
promise may continue. Abraham initiates an action that develops into a charming love story.
There is ample room within the plan of God for
the tension of suspense and the delights of ro-
mance.

What fulfilled promise do you find being
worked out in your life?

PRAYER: Merciful and kind God, you order the
sweep of history, mighty in origins and grand in
ends. You also attend to personal details: the trust-
worthiness of a servant, the choice of a spouse. I
praise you for your presence and guidance in all
things large and small. Amen.

"Grant Me Success Today"
READ Genesis 24:10–21

And he said, "O LORD, God of my master
Abraham, please grant me success today
and show steadfast love to my master
Abraham."

Genesis 24:12

The servant was conscious that he was working
in the middle of God's working. God's providence
was the large context in which he was carrying
out his duty. There are no accidents in such lives.
Every detail is luminous: the prayer, the appearance of Rebekah, the exact words spoken, the si-
lent attentiveness.

What do you know of Rebekah?

PRAYER: Too often, God, I work grudgingly and
unbelievingly. I don't think my tasks have dignity
or importance. But over and over you show me
that everything makes a difference, that no task is
too menial to be significant in the salvation you
are working out in the world today. *Amen.*

"Come in"

READ Genesis 24:22–33

He said, "Come in, O blessed of the LORD.
Why do you stand outside when I have
prepared the house and a place for the
camels?"

Genesis 24:31

Everything depends here on actual encounter:
Abraham's message delivered to the right person,
the right person responding to the message. The
ritual of hospitality, carefully described, provides
the setting for recognition and meeting.

How is hospitality important in your life?

PRAYER: Lord Jesus Christ, you met people where
they were and made them feel welcome. Be with
me today so that every meeting becomes an act of
honest speaking and true listening, gracious acceptance and courteous service. Amen.

"The Thing Comes from the Lord"

READ Genesis 24:34–51

Then Laban and Bethuel answered, "The
thing comes from the LORD; we cannot
speak to you anything bad or good.
Look, Rebekah is before you, take her
and go, and let her be the wife of your
master's son, as the LORD has spoken."

Genesis 24:50–51

As the servant tells his story it is evident that
prayer is at the heart of the experience: he prayed
for guidance, he received direction, he bowed and
worshiped. This deep-rootedness in petition and
adoration shapes the narrative.

Is prayer at the heart or at the edge of your life?

PRAYER: God Almighty, sometimes prayer, for me,
is an afterthought, something tacked on to what I
have already planned on my own. I want it to be
deep and central, the essential intimacy with you
that shapes everything I do and say. *Amen.*

"I Will"

READ Genesis 24:52–61

And they called Rebekah, and said to her,
    "Will you go with this man?" She said,
    "I will."

Genesis 24:58

Up to this point the narrative has been leisurely.
Nothing has been hurried, nothing rushed. But
now that God's hand is clearly revealed, delay is
intolerable, procrastination unthinkable.

Do you procrastinate?

PRAYER: Train me, Christ, in sensitivity to your
ways so that I will sense when to go slowly and
when to act quickly, when relaxed waiting is
called for and when immediate obedience is necessary. Amen.

"Rebekah Looked up"

READ Genesis 24:62–67

And Rebekah looked up, and when she
saw Isaac, she slipped quickly from the
camel. . . .

Genesis 24:64

Isaac and Rebekah meet at the point at which their
eyes are "looking up." The phrase combines elements of expectation and adoration. Isaac's evening meditation and Rebekah's prompt obedience
have made them ready for this marriage.

What are you looking forward to?

PRAYER: God of hope and God of glory, I will keep
alert and expectant through this day for the evidence of your blessing. I will keep open and wor-
shipful for the reception of your grace. Guide
these intentions and sustain them by your Spirit.
Amen.

APRIL 11

"Full of Years"

READ Genesis 25:1–11

Abraham breathed his last and died in a
good old age, an old man and full of
years, and was gathered to his people.

Genesis 25:8

Our ancestors talked of dying "a good death."
Abraham's death is presented as good: an accepted
completion. His part in the pilgrimage is complete;
his burial plot is prepared; his sons Isaac and
Ishmael preside over the burial rites.

Do you think of your own death in these terms?

PRAYER: "Teach me to live, that I may dread the
grave as little as my bed; teach me to die, that I
may rise glorious at the Judgment Day" (Thomas
Ken, "All Praise to Thee, My God, This Night," in
The Hymnbook, p. 63). Amen.

"Descendants of Ishmael"

READ Genesis 25:12–18

These are the descendants of Ishmael,
    Abraham's son, whom Hagar the
    Egyptian, Sarah's slave-girl, bore to
    Abraham.

Genesis 25:12

The salvation story of covenant promise is told through Isaac. But that does not mean that Ishmael has no story. Even though Ishmael's story is not told, it is interesting that he is not ignored. His presence is affirmed and his descendants accounted for.

What is significant about Ishmael for you?

PRAYER: Father in heaven, help me to be content to know that Ishmael is included in your plan without having to know *how* he is part of your plan. Defend me against distracting curiosities and diverting questions. Lead me in the way of trust and obedience. *Amen.*

"Rebekah His Wife Conceived"
READ Genesis 25:19–26

Isaac prayed to the LORD for his wife,
    because she was barren; and the LORD
    granted his prayer, and his wife Rebekah
    conceived.

Genesis 25:21

Isaac was forty when he married, sixty when he became a father. People of faith wait a lot. We admire the results of faith but we don't want to participate in the process of faith. Yet the years of barrenness are as much an experience of faith as moments of conception and birth.

What are you waiting for?

PRAYER: I immerse myself in your eternity and grace, Almighty God. I want to enter the rhythms of your covenant, sensitive to the timing of mercy, watchful for the surprises of resurrection. Keep me from haste or panic, in the name of Jesus, who came in the fullness of time. Amen.

APRIL 14

"Esau/Isaac"

READ Genesis 25:27–28

Isaac loved Esau, because he was fond of
game; but Rebekah loved Jacob.

Genesis 25:28

The twin boys develop in contrast: they struggle
in the womb, they are born in conflict, they grow
in divergent directions. The differences are deep-
ened by parental favoritism. Do contrasts necessarily become oppositions?

What conflicting forces do you deal with?

PRAYER: I am aware, Lord God, that I am born into
conflict. I do not enter a world of harmony but
one of strife. I do not find everyone agreed on
what is best for me, but experience contradictory
counsel. Lead me through the conflicts to the clarity of covenant and grace. Amen.

"Thus Esau Despised His Birthright"
READ Genesis 25:29–34

Then Jacob gave Esau bread and lentil
stew, and he ate and drank, and rose and
went his way. Thus Esau despised his
birthright.

Genesis 25:34

The contrast between the brothers is extended
now to their characters, which become their des-
tinies. Esau is hungry and will not wait; Jacob is
willing to wait. Pottage gives immediate gratification; the birthright involves waiting for fulfillment.

Who are you most like, Jacob or Esau?

PRAYER: I am too much in a hurry, God. I greedily
want everything in life, and I want it now. I know
that you want all things for me, but I forget that
the times of fulfillment are in your hands. Help
me to be as trustful of your timing as I am de-
sirous of your blessing. Amen.

APRIL 16

"Isaac Went to Gerar"

READ Genesis 26:1–5

Now there was a famine in the land,
   besides the former famine that had
   occurred in the days of Abraham. And
   Isaac went to Gerar, to King Abimelech
   of the Philistines.

Genesis 26:1

Faced with a threat to his survival, Isaac's first response was to look for help from a human being
(Abimelech). But God calls him back to faith.
Isaac has to learn that he cannot ride on his father's covenant coattails; he also must live by faith.

Where is Gerar?

PRAYER: Thank you, faithful God, for the reaffir-
mations of your promises to me: the assurance of
your blessing, the expressions of your love, the
relentlessness of your guidance, the clarity of
your covenant. All thanks, through Jesus Christ.
Amen.

"He Was Afraid"

READ Genesis 26:6–16

When the men of the place asked him
about his wife, he said, "She is my
sister"; for he was afraid to say, "My
wife," thinking, "or else the men of the
place might kill me for the sake of
Rebekah, because she is attractive in
appearance."

Genesis 26:7

Isaac not only entered into the covenant that God
made with his father, he repeated the sins of his
father (Genesis 12:10–20; 20:1–18). The generations get no better! The theme, though, is not
human progress (there is none) but God's faithfulness, which finds expression in Isaac's prosperity.

What is the character of Abimelech?

PRAYER: Dear God, I confess my anxiety-provoked
sins, my fear-induced wrongdoings. Your word is
steady and true, my word is fickle and false. Forgive me and restore me to the joy of your salvation. Amen.

APRIL 18

"Isaac Dug Again the Wells"
READ Genesis 26:17–25

Isaac dug again the wells of water that
   had been dug in the days of his father
   Abraham; for the Philistines had stopped
   them up after the death of Abraham. . . .
                        Genesis 26:18a

The sources of life-giving water were clogged with junk. Isaac cannot live off of what Abraham did; he has to redo it himself. The life of faith is like that. Philistine trash pollutes and stops the flow of life. The wells of faith have to be cleaned up and new wells dug.

What well-digging projects are you involved in?

PRAYER: God Almighty, there is so much human garbage that gets in the way of my sources in you. Keep me from giving up or giving in, so that I am energetic in digging through the refuse, daily reaching the wellspring of my life in Christ. Amen.

"Abimelech . . . Esau"

READ Genesis 26:26–35

Then Abimelech went to him from Gerar,
with Ahuzzath his adviser and Phicol the
commander of his army.

Genesis 26:26

The outsider Abimelech seeks to make a treaty
with Isaac; Isaac's own son Esau later makes life
bitter for him. One sees God's blessing and wants
to get in on it; the other sees God's blessing and is
resentful of it. God's blessing does not always get
a positive response.

Do you ever respond resentfully to signs of
God's blessing?

PRAYER: You, O God, are generous with your
blessings. Sometimes I am more aware of them in
others than in myself and am provoked to jealousy. Forgive me for my small-mindedness, my
mean-spiritedness, and help me to rejoice in what
you do, wherever and in whomever you do it.
Amen.

APRIL 20

"Prepare for Me Savory Food"

READ Genesis 27:1–17

"Then prepare for me savory food, such as
I like, and bring it to me to eat, so that I
may bless you before I die."

Genesis 27:4

The four family members engage in a tense inter-
play of wills that sets the father's will to bless the
elder son against the mother's strategy to bless the
younger son. God's promises get tangled up with
human scheming!

What is the difference between Isaac and
Rebekah?

PRAYER: Lord God, your plan is so clear and positive but my participation in it is so flawed. I marvel that you get anything accomplished! Chasten
my desires and purge my deceits as you fulfill
your will, through Jesus Christ my Lord. *Amen.*

"And Blessed Him"

READ Genesis 27:18–29

So he came near and kissed him; and he
smelled the smell of his garments, and
blessed him. . . .

Genesis 27:27a

Rebekah's stratagem works: Jacob is blessed. The mixture of the father's blessing and the mother's duplicity is used to do God's will. But there is more here than the father's intent and the mother's cunning. God's blessing is being worked out.

Compare the blessing with the prophecy in Genesis 25:23.

PRAYER: Almighty God, eternal in power, steadfast in mercy, you work with such fragile stuff—the words and gestures, the intents and deceits of parents and children. And out of it you bring blessing! All glory to your name! *Amen.*

"Is He Not Rightly Named Jacob?"

READ Genesis 27:30–40

Esau said, "Is he not rightly named Jacob?"

Genesis 27:36a

This passage is full of pathos: the anguish of Isaac in being deceived, the bitterness of Esau in being defrauded. The father and son are united in their suffering. No one wants to live an unblessed life.

What does "Jacob" mean?

PRAYER: I see much that seems to me unjust in the world, God, much that offends my sense of fairness. Can you bring blessing and salvation out of this suffering? Will you? I trust myself to your love and will. Amen.

"Esau Hated Jacob"

Genesis 27:41–45

Now Esau hated Jacob because of the
blessing with which his father had
blessed him, and Esau said to himself,
"The days of mourning for my father are
approaching; then I will kill my brother
Jacob."

Genesis 27:41

The story is narrated in such a way that our sym-
pathies are enlisted on the side of Isaac and Esau
and against Rebekah and Jacob. But these sympa-
thies are not a reliable means for searching out the
mysteries of God.

What in life right now are you puzzled over?

PRAYER: "God moves in a mysterious way His
wonders to perform; He plants His footsteps in
the sea, and rides upon the storm. Deep in un-
fathomable mines of never-failing skill He treasures up His bright designs, and works His
sovereign will" (William Cowper, "God Moves in
a Mysterious Way," in *The Hymnbook*, p. 112). *Amen.*

"Take as a Wife"

Go at once to Paddan-aram to the house of
  Bethuel, your mother's father; and take
  as wife from there one of the daughters
  of Laban, your mother's brother.

Genesis 28:2

No one person—not Abraham, not Isaac, not
Jacob, not Esau—provides a complete exposition
of the life of faith. The blessing is international
and intergenerational. The getting of wives is an
important part of the story, linking families and
making families.

To whom are you linked in the life of faith?

PRAYER: Eternal Father, I thank you for the extensive and diverse family into which I am introduced
in the life of faith. Unlikely persons become brothers and sisters; untold figures become mothers
and fathers. "Here is your son! Here is your
mother!" Amen.

APRIL 25

"A Ladder"

READ Genesis 28:10–22

And he dreamed that there was a ladder set
up on the earth, the top of it reaching to
heaven; and the angels of God were
ascending and descending on it.

Genesis 28:12

Jacob's night dream at Bethel is a brilliant insight
into the daylight reality of faith: there is constant
traffic between earth and heaven; God is near when
we are aware of his presence and when we are
not; the ordinary is the gate to the extraordinary.

How do you evaluate Jacob's vow?

PRAYER: "Though like the wanderer, the sun gone
down, darkness be over me, my rest a stone; yet
in my dreams I'd be nearer, my God, to Thee.
There let the way appear steps unto heaven: all
that Thou sendest me in mercy given: angels to
beckon me nearer, my God, to Thee" (Sarah F.
Adams, "Nearer, My God, to Thee," in The Hymnbook, p. 326). Amen.

"Then Jacob Kissed Rachel"

READ Genesis 29:1–14

Then Jacob kissed Rachel, and wept aloud.

Genesis 29:11

Jacob's entrance into the territory and family of Laban is marked by recognition and affection. The presence of Jacob always introduces conflict, but the conflict is played out in a context of covenant and blessing.

Compare this with the visit of the servant in Genesis 24.

PRAYER: Wherever I go I find persons prepared for greetings and blessing, O God. I thank you for this family of faith that sets me in immediate and intimate relationship with persons of strange language and culture, bound as we are by your commands and love. Amen.

"Two Daughters"

READ *Genesis* 29:15–30

Now Laban had two daughters; the name
of the elder was Leah, and the name of
the younger was Rachel.

Genesis 29:16

Conflict, which erupted in the twins Jacob and
Esau, now casts its shadow on the daughters Leah
and Rachel as they become wives to Jacob. The
seeds of duplicity that Jacob sowed earlier are now
being reaped in a conflict in his own marriage.

Which aspects of this story are tragic? Which
are comic?

PRAYER: I need your mercy, O God, every step of
the way. The consequences of earlier sins keep
intruding themselves into the present. Without
daily grace I would not find my way to the blessing promised and given in Jesus Christ. *Amen.*

APRIL 28

"He Opened Her Womb"

READ *Genesis 29:31–35*

When the LORD saw that Leah was unloved,
he opened her womb; but Rachel was
barren.

Genesis 29:31

The oft-admired love story between Jacob and
Rachel obscures the pathos of Leah's unrequited
love. Her four sons are named in praise of God's
love, which sustained her, and in hope of a husband's love, which she never experienced.

How have you been disappointed in love?

PRAYER: Your love, O God, is strong and eternal. I
receive it and I share it. But I do not always have it
returned by those whom I love. Some ignore me.
Some reject me. Sustain me in these losses and increase the fruitfulness of my love from and for
you. *Amen.*

"God Remembered Rachel"

READ Genesis 30:1–24

Then God remembered Rachel, and God
heeded her and opened her womb.

Genesis 30:22

The childbearing competition verges on the com-
ical, each wife striving to outdo the other whether
by maid or by mandrake. Yet out of such flawed
motives are born the leaders who form the tribes
of Israel. God shapes good out of our embarrass-
ingly unworthy lives.

What does your name mean?

PRAYER: These stories remind me, Father, that neither the circumstances of my conception nor the
motives of my parents determine my life. It is
your design for me and your love in me that matter. Work out your salvation in my life as I receive
your love and respond to your call in Christ. *Amen.*

"Name Your Wages"

READ Genesis 30:25–43

> But Laban said to him, "If you will allow me
> to say so, I have learned by divination that
> the LORD has blessed me because of you;
> name your wages, and I will give it."
>
> Genesis 30:27–28

Laban and Jacob compete for superiority. They
are both aware of God's providence but are so
absorbed in their own schemes for getting the
better of each other that the awareness does not
shape their actions.

How does your belief in God shape the way
you do your daily work?

PRAYER: God, I want what I believe about you to
form the way I work for you. I want my belief and
my behavior to be integrated so that I live with
ease, with trust, with generous openness. *Amen.*

"Return to the Land"

READ Genesis 31:1–21

Then the LORD said to Jacob, "Return to
the land of your ancestors and to your
kindred, and I will be with you."

Genesis 31:3

The call of God reasserts itself. Like the call to
Abraham, it requires an abrupt departure. Jacob
refers to God's leadership three times (vv. 5, 7, 9)
as he draws the daughters of Laban into this fresh
venture in pilgrimage.

What new directions in pilgrimage do you
sense in your life?

PRAYER: Almighty God, don't let me get so settled
into prosperous routines that I am unable or un-
willing to hear and respond to your call to the life
in which Jesus Christ leads me. *Amen.*

"Why Did You Flee Secretly?"

READ Genesis 31:22–42

"Why did you flee secretly and deceive me
and not tell me? I would have sent you
away with mirth and songs, with
tambourine and lyre."

Genesis 31:27

Jacob fled from Esau his brother; now he flees from Laban his father-in-law. Somehow he does not endear himself to those with whom he lives! But even when he is running away, he runs into the covenant design of God that shapes his life.

When have you run away from a bad situation?

PRAYER: Father in heaven, you use not only my hopes, also my fears to motivate me and get me where you want me. Even when I act in cowardice, you turn my weakness into an experience of grace, for which I give you deep thanks. *Amen.*

MAY 3

"The Pillar Mizpah"
READ Genesis 31:43–55

Therefore he called it Galeed, and the pillar
Mizpah, for he said, "The LORD watch
between you and me, when we are
absent one from the other."

Genesis 31:48b–49

This story, tense with the rivalry, anger, and suspi-
cion of Jacob and Laban, develops into a story
about God who is between them and over both of
them. There is a will greater than their own that
determines their existence.

What does "Mizpah" mean?

PRAYER: I commit myself, faithful God, to your
watchful care. I also commit the lives of those I
fear and those I love to your rule. Keep us all in
the way of salvation, through Christ our Lord.
Amen.

"Perhaps He Will Accept Me"

READ Genesis 32:1–21

> For he thought, "I may appease him with
> the present that goes ahead of me, and
> afterwards I shall see his face; perhaps he
> will accept me."
>
> Genesis 32:20b

There is something pathetic about this elaborate
stratagem: Jacob, feeling guilty for defrauding his
brother and fearful for his life, hopes to bribe
Esau with lavish gifts. Unacceptable as a person,
he hopes to buy acceptance with his possessions.

Do you ever use gifts as bribes?

PRAYER: God, I have learned that nothing I bring
to you can atone for my sin, but that your Son has
done it for me. I come to you not fearfully, not
guiltily, but blessed and confident in Jesus' name!
Amen.

"God Face to Face"

So Jacob called the place Peniel, saying,
   "For I have seen God face to face, and
   yet my life is preserved."

Genesis 32:30

Jacob thought that his next struggle would be with Esau. He was wrong. It was with God. Jacob had spent his life getting the best of others; now God gets the best of him. Jacob comes out of the encounter blessed but wounded.

What is the nature of your struggle with God?

PRAYER: I don't want to spend my life running from one failure to another, O God, or even from one success to another; I want to meet you, face to face. Change me and bless me, so I can live to your glory. Amen.

"He Bought"

READ *Genesis* 33:1–20

And from the sons of Hamor, Shechem's
father, he bought for one hundred pieces
of money the plot of land on which he
had pitched his tent.

Genesis 33:19

After reconciliation with his brother, Jacob sets
himself to live openly and responsibly with the
Canaanites. No more cheating. No more trickery.
He buys land and builds an altar. Honest before
men and God!

Locate Succoth and Shechem.

PRAYER: Dear God, I want the things I learn in
struggle and obedience with you to make my life
with my neighbors better: considerate, straight-
forward, trustworthy. I want my business activities and my worship activities to be in harmony.
Amen.

"Dinah"

READ Genesis 34:1–17

Now Jacob heard that Shechem had defiled
his daughter Dinah; but his sons were
with his cattle in the field, so Jacob held
his peace until they came.

Genesis 34:5

Jacob's peaceful new life in Canaan is interrupted
by the rape of Dinah. Is it going to be possible for
these two peoples to live side by side? Morality,
economics, and religion, the classic issues that
separate people, are introduced into this already
tense drama.

What is Hamor's main point of appeal?

PRAYER: I know, Lord, that it is not easy to live in
community. Violence, rudeness, ignorance, self-
indulgence all play havoc with relationships. In
this complex and difficult society, reinforce my
determination to live in love, and increase my
wisdom in how to do it. *Amen.*

"Only Let Us Agree with Them"

READ *Genesis* 34:18–31

"Will not their livestock, their property,
and all their animals be ours? Only let us
agree with them, and they will live
among us."

Genesis 34:23

The Shechemites were willing to use the religious rite of circumcision to get an economic advantage. The Israelites used it as a cloak for their seething vengeance. Both were "using" religion, both involved in a horrible sacrilege.

Is Jacob any better motivated here than his sons?

PRAYER: As I pick my way through this morally chaotic society in which I live, Holy God, I find very few people to guide me, almost no one to look up to who can give light to my path. Jesus, show me the way, the truth, and the life. *Amen.*

"Bethel"

READ *Genesis* 35:1–15

> God said to Jacob, "Arise, go up to Bethel,
> and settle there. Make an altar there to
> the God who appeared to you when you
> fled from your brother Esau."
>
> *Genesis* 35:1

Jacob returns to the place where his pilgrimage began. A circuit is complete: flight, return, acceptance. The covenant promise is repeated and the place of worship established. God has not changed, but what changes have taken place in Jacob, newly named Israel!

Compare this with the earlier experience at Bethel (Genesis 28).

PRAYER: "O God of Bethel, by whose hand Thy people still are fed; who through this weary pilgrimage hast all our fathers led. O spread Thy covering wings around till all our wanderings cease, and at our Father's loved abode our souls arrive in peace" (P. Doddridge, "O God of Bethel," in *The Hymnbook*, p. 342). *Amen.*

"Rachel Died"

READ Genesis 35:16–29

So Rachel died, and she was buried on the
way to Ephrath (that is, Bethlehem). . . .

Genesis 35:19

Rachel gives birth to the twelfth son of Isaac and
dies. Isaac dies a short time later. It is the end of an
era. The twelve tribes of Israel enter the stream of
history bearing the covenant commitments established in these great patriarchal families.

Why did Jacob change his son's name?

PRAYER: As I return to these stories time after
time, O Lord, searching for the meaning of my
life and the direction of your love, keep me attentive and obedient to every new insight that you
open up to me by your Spirit. *Amen.*

"Descendants of Esau"

READ *Genesis* 36:1–40

> These are the descendants of Esau, ancestor
> of the Edomites, in the hill country of Seir.
>
> *Genesis* 36:9

Family lists are not the most exciting or inspiring reading. There are no sermon texts in this chapter. But the lists are important, all the same. Esau, rejected as the covenant bearer, is not rejected as a person; he and all his heirs are included in the history of the community of faith.

What is most attractive to you about Esau?

PRAYER: Father in heaven, give breadth to my vision of your salvation so that I can recognize your great generosity, gathering in the rejected, naming the left out, and bringing them to acknowledge your lordship, even in Jesus Christ. *Amen.*

MAY 12

"The Family of Jacob"

READ Genesis 37:1–24

Jacob settled in the land where his father
had lived as an alien, the land of Canaan.
This is the story of the family of Jacob.

Genesis 37:1–2a

The narrative shifts from the brother of Jacob
(Esau) to the sons of Jacob. One son, Joseph, car-
ries the story. His father's love for him and his
brothers' hatred of him provide the human dimensions for this exploration of the way God
keeps covenant with us.

How does jealousy work in your life?

PRAYER: Why is it so difficult, dear God, for me to
be spontaneously glad when I see you use and
bless another? Why am I so often grudging in my
feelings? Forgive me for these insidious jealousies
and purge me of them, so that I can praise you
with a glad heart. Amen.

"They Took Joseph to Egypt"
READ Genesis 37:25–36

When some Midianite traders passed by,
    they drew Joseph up, lifting him out of
    the pit, and sold him to the Ishmaelites
    for twenty pieces of silver. And they took
    Joseph to Egypt.

Genesis 37:28

It is difficult to imagine a worse beginning for
Joseph or a worse ending for Jacob. Can anything
good come out of this? We know that it does.
The story of salvation specializes in impossible
conditions.

What is the most difficult fact in your life right
now?

PRAYER: Lord God, I pray that I may not be over-
whelmed when I become aware of the cruelties
that people let loose on each other, whether in
families or in nations. Keep me attentive to the
place in the story where you are working salvation. *Amen.*

"Tamar"

READ Genesis 38:1–30

Then Judah said to his daughter-in-law
    Tamar, "Remain a widow in your
    father's house until my son Shelah grows
    up"—for he feared that he too would
    die, like his brothers.

Genesis 38:11a

The story of faith takes a special interest in the poor and the exploited. Tamar enters the story as a widow who is being deprived of her rights by her father-in-law, Judah. Oblivious to faults in himself, Judah is quick to hand out a death verdict on Tamar. But he is implicated in his own judgment. To his credit, he recognizes it.

Consider the significance of Matthew 1:3 in the genealogy of Jesus.

PRAYER: Holy God, instead of looking around me and searching for what others are doing wrong, I need the courage to examine my own heart and detect the sins that separate me from you and diminish the people with whom I live. Amen.

"His Master's Wife"
READ *Genesis* 39:1–18

And after a time his master's wife cast her
eyes on Joseph and said, "Lie with me."

Genesis 39:7

Is Joseph successful because he is quick to meet
people's expectations of him, or because he is
centered in God's will for him? His character is
tested. Joseph, clearly, is no opportunist. Afflic-
tion brings out the best in him. All through his
life, Joseph will get his identity not from where
he is but from who is with him.

How has your character been put to the test?

PRAYER: I want to do well with my life, Father, but
on your terms, not the world's. Give me courage
to reject the seductions of the world and the ambition of my own ego, and to live by your daily
grace and mercy. *Amen.*

"Prison"

READ *Genesis 39:19–23*

And Joseph's master took him and put
him into the prison, the place where
the king's prisoners were confined; he
remained there in prison.

Genesis 39:20

The external conditions of Joseph's life changed
radically; the internal reality (God's presence, prosperity) was constant. Places (the pit in Dothan,
Potiphar's house, this prison) vary in comfort but
are equally useful for God's purposes.

Use Romans 8:37–39 to meditate on this.

PRAYER: I spend far too much time worrying
about where I am and not enough thinking about
whom I am with, O God. It is your presence that
makes the difference, not my location. Show me
how to participate in your purposes in every place
I find myself today. *Amen.*

"We Have Had Dreams"
READ Genesis 40:1–8

They said to him, "We have had dreams,
and there is no one to interpret them."
And Joseph said to them, "Do not interpretations belong to God? Please tell
them to me."

Genesis 40:8

The prison population grows. New prisoners get drawn into the life of salvation. Joseph, alert to the working of God in palace and prison, in waking thoughts and sleeping dreams, is quick to offer the disturbing dreams of the butler and baker to God's use.

What makes you downcast?

PRAYER: Lead me, Lord, into a comprehensive, embracing attentiveness to your working. I don't want to miss anything—opportunities for service, signs of distress in a friend's face—that may provide a way for sharing your love. Amen.

"Interpretation"

READ Genesis 40:9–19

Then Joseph said to him, "This is its
   interpretation. . . ."

Genesis 40:12a

Joseph interprets the dreams of the butler and
baker. The future is bright for one, dark for the
other. The interpretations are gifts, providing
both men time to prepare themselves in freedom
for life and death, rather than to exist merely as
playthings of fate.

How do you face the future: with hope or with
resignation?

PRAYER: God of hope, you have told me enough
about the future that I know you are in it and that
my part in it is to continue to live in obedient and
expectant faith. Give me the courage to do so.
Amen.

"Did Not Remember Joseph"

READ Genesis 40:20–23

Yet the chief cupbearer did not remember
Joseph, but forgot him.

Genesis 40:23

The butler's forgetfulness is endemic to the
human condition. We get so absorbed in our own
fortunes or failures that we exclude from awareness anyone who is not immediately present, anyone who is not at this moment necessary to us.

What key person do you systematically exclude
from your life?

PRAYER: How severely my life is diminished by
forgetfulness, God. And how sad that I diminish
the lives of others at the same time. Forgive me for
my thoughtless preoccupation with my own affairs and my forgetful indifference to the needs of
others. *Amen.*

"I Remember My Faults Today"

READ Genesis 41:1–13

Then the chief cupbearer said to Pharaoh,
"I remember my faults today."

Genesis 41:9

Two years of forgetfulness are interrupted by
Pharaoh's uninterpreted dreams. The forgetful
butler remembers. He remembers not only
Joseph's interpretive gift but also his own failure
to keep his promise to Joseph. His confession of
sin opens the way for renewal of life.

What unremembered faults can you call to
remembrance?

PRAYER: I have a keen memory for grievances,
Lord, but a poor one for gratitude. I have a hard
time forgetting wrongs against me, a hard time
remembering the rights provided me. Help me to
remember my faults instead of the faults of others.
Amen.

"No One So Discerning and Wise"
READ Genesis 41:14—45

So Pharaoh said to Joseph, "Since God has
shown you all this, there is no one so
discerning and wise as you."

Genesis 41:39

Joseph is restored to favor, this time with authority over the entire land of Egypt. Pharaoh's dreams
become the vehicle for bringing Joseph's wisdom
out into the open. Egyptian ways of knowing fail,
and God's way of revealing emerges preeminent.

Who do you know who is "discerning and
wise"?

PRAYER: All-wise God, the world is in confusion
and disarray as information accumulates and there
is no one to interpret it. Give me, along with all
people of faith, wisdom to lead my friends and
neighbors to live wisely by the vision you provide
in Jesus Christ. Amen.

"All"

READ Genesis 41:46–57

Moreover, all the world came to Joseph in
Egypt to buy grain, because the famine
became severe throughout the world.

Genesis 41:57

The repeated emphasis of "all" is not accidental
but designed to show the sovereignty of God's
blessing working through Joseph. The totalitarian
Egyptian state is a failure; the total rule of God expressed in Joseph brings wholeness.

How many times is the word "all" used?

PRAYER: My God and King, instead of trying to establish my own famine-cursed rule, I will accept
your prosperity-marked rule, in Jesus Christ. *Amen.*

MAY 26

"Go Again. God Almighty Grant You Mercy"
READ *Genesis 43:1–15*

". . . may God Almighty grant you mercy
before the man, so that he may send
back your other brother and Benjamin.
As for me, if I am bereaved of my
children, I am bereaved."

Genesis 43:14

When pushed to the wall Jacob is a man of faith,
ready to risk everything on God's mercy. His sons,
despite their promises, have proved themselves
unreliable. His God, as it turns out, proves faithful.
What people have most disappointed you?

PRAYER: Dear God, without thinking I transfer my
distrust of people to you. What I want is to let my
trust in your faithful ways get transferred into
human relationships, so that I, and my family and
friends, get caught up in the completion of your
covenant with us. *Amen.*

MAY 23

"And Joseph's Brothers Came"
READ *Genesis 42:1–17*

Now Joseph was governor over the land; it
was he who sold to all the people of the
land. And Joseph's brothers came and
bowed themselves before him with their
faces to the ground.

Genesis 42:6

The scene shifts from Joseph and the empire to
Joseph and his brothers. They come to him full of
anxiety and drenched in guilt. They need not only
bread, but also mercy. Will they get it?
How have the brothers changed?

PRAYER: Lord, you are merciful and gracious, but
when I am harassed by guilt and plagued by anxiety I have a difficult time perceiving who you are,
how you act. Forgive me and reconcile me, for
Jesus' sake. *Amen.*

MAY 24

"We Are Paying the Penalty"
READ *Genesis* 42:18–28

They said to one another, "Alas, we are
paying the penalty for what we did to
our brother; we saw his anguish when
he pleaded with us, but we would not
listen. That is why this anguish has come
upon us."

Genesis 42:21

Guilty sinners experience both judgment and
mercy as providence develops in their lives: making Simeon hostage was a severe judgment; re-
placing the money was a kindly mercy.

How are judgments and mercies interconnected
in your life?

PRAYER: "Lead, kindly Light, amid th' encircling
gloom, lead Thou me on; the night is dark, and I
am far from home; lead Thou me on: keep Thou
my feet; I do not ask to see the distant scene—
one step enough for me" (John Henry Newman,
"Lead, Kindly Light," in *The Hymnbook*, p. 331).
Amen.

MAY 25

"With Sorrow to Sheol"
READ *Genesis* 42:29–38

"If harm should come to him on the
journey that you are to make, you would
bring down my gray hairs with sorrow
to Sheol."

Genesis 42:38b

Jacob is in the middle of one of the great stories of
salvation, but he doesn't know it. All he can think
of is his loss. Deceived and bereft, he is no longer
living by faith or in hope. For as long as he continues this way, the story cannot develop.

Compare this speech of Reuben with that in
Genesis 37:22.

PRAYER: Almighty God, how much do I miss
every day in my inattentive unbelief? I let my dis-
appointment with people crowd out my faith in
your providence. Help me to see through human
lies and failures to your truth and salvation. *Amen.*

"Overcome with Affection"

READ Genesis 43:16–34

With that, Joseph hurried out, because he
was overcome with affection for his
brother, and he was about to weep. So
he went into a private room and wept
there.

Genesis 43:30

Joseph has been in control to this point. He has
treated the brothers with impersonal coolness.
Now passion breaks out. He is no longer the effi-
cient administrator but the heartbroken brother.
God's mercy betrays him into extravagance.

What is behind Joseph's special feeling for Benjamin?

PRAYER: Merciful and loving Father, I can never
calculate your blessings, never account for the
movements of grace. You surprise me with new
elements, unguessed fulfillments. All praise! All
thanks! In Jesus' name. *Amen.*

"The Cup"

READ Genesis 44:1–17

He searched, beginning with the eldest and
ending with the youngest; and the cup
was found in Benjamin's sack.

Genesis 44:12

The brothers are subjected to severe stress. In the
testing they realize and confess their guilt (v. 16).
At this extremity they are in a position to experience grace, for it is grace, not grain, that they
most need.

What stresses prepare you for grace?

PRAYER: I dare, O God, to thank you for the ex-
tremities that prove that there is no way out but
through you. I don't want my life to be a patch-
work of halfhearted resolutions and fitful promises; I want it to be wholehearted repentance and
a committed faith. Amen.

"How Can I Go Back?"

READ Genesis 44:18–34

"For how can I go back to my father if the
   boy is not with me? I fear to see the
   suffering that would come upon my
   father."

Genesis 44:34

Joseph appears to be playing a cat-and-mouse
game: Benjamin is in jeopardy; Judah and the brothers are terrified; the father waits at a distance in
anxiety and ignorance. Guilt from the past and fear
of evil reach a saturation point in the narrative.

What is the worst time you have ever experienced?

PRAYER: God, you give songs in the night, you
make streams in the desert. No matter how closed
in I feel, no matter how fearful I become, keep me
aware that my tremors cannot measure the Om-
nipotence. *Amen.*

"God Sent Me Before You"

READ Genesis 45:1–28

"And now do not be distressed, or angry
with yourselves, because you sold me
here; for God sent me before you to
preserve life."

Genesis 45:5

Joseph's self-disclosure is stunning in two dimensions: the brothers thought that he was dead, and he is alive; they thought that their sin and guilt had bungled life irreparably, but all along God was shaping salvation. Joseph, unexpectedly alive, is God's means of countering the famine-diminished life, the sorrow-weakened life, the guilt-crippled life. Poverty and alienation are banished in this resurrection festival.

Note the repetitions, "God sent," in verses 5, 7, and 8.

PRAYER: Open my eyes, O God, to your presence and action in my life, so that I can see how you are active in preserving life and providing salvation in the midst of the world's violence and rebellion. *Amen.*

"Jacob, Jacob"

READ Genesis 46:1–27

God spoke to Israel in visions of the night, and
said, "Jacob, Jacob." And he said, "Here I am."
Then he said, "I am God, the God of your
father; do not be afraid to go down to Egypt,
for I will make of you a great nation there."

Genesis 46:2–3

Earlier trips to Egypt were made in unbelief; this
one is made in belief. Joseph's invitation is not
enough for Jacob; the reassurances of his sons are
not enough. God's word must confirm the action,
authorizing the sojourn in Egypt. The naming of
the seventy emphasizes the extent of the blessing
from God's side—everyone is included. It also
emphasizes the extent of faith from Jacob's side—
no one is left behind for security; all are risked in
this new venture into the unknown.

What is the difference between Jacob's and
Abraham's trip to Egypt?

PRAYER: Eternal God, no matter how clear your
word has been in the past, I need it spoken in
fresh ways for this day's journey. Repeat the promises, so that I can travel today with assurance and
clarity in the way of Jesus Christ my Lord. *Amen.*

"The Land of Goshen"

READ Genesis 46:28–34

Israel sent Judah ahead to Joseph to lead
the way before him into Goshen. When
they came to the land of Goshen, Joseph
made ready his chariot and went up to
meet his father Israel in Goshen.

Genesis 46:28–29a

Arrangements are made for an Egyptian sojourn
in such a way that the sojourners' identity is preserved. Important as Egypt is to them, they will
not become Egyptians. They will maintain their
distinctive way of life out of the mainstream, in
the borderland of Goshen.

Where is Goshen?

PRAYER: Eternal God, show me how to live in the
world without becoming of the world. I want to
live responsibly and gratefully in this community;
but I don't want to adopt its values or live by its
creeds. Amen.

"Joseph Provided"

READ Genesis 47:1–12

And Joseph provided his father, his
brothers, and all his father's household
with food, according to the number of
their dependents.

Genesis 47:12

"Provide" is a key word in the Joseph story. God
provides for Joseph and uses Joseph to provide for
the Egyptians, his brothers, and his father. Things
don't just happen. Life is not random. A gracious
will is at work on our behalf.

How do you experience providence?

PRAYER: "God of our life, through all the circling
years, we trust in Thee; in all the past, through all
our hopes and fears, Thy hand we see. With each
new day, when morning lifts the veil, we own Thy
mercies, Lord, which never fail" (Hugh T. Kerr,
"God of Our Life, Through All the Circling Years,"
in The Hymnbook, p. 108). Amen.

"The Famine Was Very Severe"

READ Genesis 47:13–26

Now there was no food in all the land, for
the famine was very severe. The land of
Egypt and the land of Canaan languished
because of the famine.

Genesis 47:13

Is Joseph compromising his life? Is he more concerned with possessions than with promise? Is he the agent of God's providence or is he consolidating Pharaoh's power? Joseph's life is suddenly questionable.

What threats do you see here to the covenant people?

PRAYER: All-wise God, I submit myself to your continual and searching guidance. I know that I cannot presume upon the experiences and wisdom of yesterday but that each step requires fresh faith and new obedience. Direct my pilgrimage today in the way of Jesus Christ. *Amen.*

"Carry Me out of Egypt"

READ *Genesis 47:27–31*

"When I lie down with my ancestors, carry
me out of Egypt and bury me in their
burial place." He answered, "I will do as
you have said."

Genesis 47:30

In Jacob, at least, there is no compromise with
Egyptian possessions. During his sojourn with
Laban he had been an acquisitive man, but now
he is entirely a man of promise, wholly detached
from the things of Egypt and committed only to
the continuities of the covenant.

Contrast Joseph and Jacob at this point.

PRAYER: Purify my life, Holy God, so that I can
readily let go of everything that keeps me from
pursuing your will for me. I want to begin each
day ready to leave all and follow you, wherever
you are leading. *Amen.*

"His Two Sons"

READ Genesis 48:1–22

After this Joseph was told, "Your father is ill." So he took with him his two sons, Manasseh and Ephraim.

Genesis 48:1

Three generations are present in this act of blessing, bound together by God's promises. There is no one-generation faith: God connects us with our past and our future. The blessing, tumbling out of the mouth of the old man, summarizes the incredible hope and promise that provide the substance to this story of faith.

Why is verse 22 important?

PRAYER: When I look for the meaning of my life, O God, I find it in these words of blessing, that you are always enduring and intruding—staying with the generations—and always introducing surprises into the plot. I always know what to expect (that you are with me); but I never know what to expect (who you will use, where you will lead). *Amen.*

"Then Jacob Called His Sons"

READ Genesis 49:1–27

Then Jacob called his sons, and said:
  "Gather around, that I may tell you what
  will happen to you in days to come."

Genesis 49:1

What is the best heritage a parent can give to a child? Is it not a hope, a blessing, a destiny? Jacob's sons are blessed with a future. Each receives an image suited to his destiny. What they have in common is a future in God's plan.

What inheritance did you receive from your parents?

PRAYER: As I ponder my place in your life of promise, Lord God, help me to hear what you speak concerning my calling, my uniqueness, my destiny as your child, my part in bearing your blessing. Amen.

"Then He Charged Them"

READ Genesis 49:28–33

Then he charged them, saying to them, "I
am about to be gathered to my people.
Bury me with my ancestors—in the cave
in the field of Ephron the Hittite. . . ."

Genesis 49:29

In his blessings the father binds his sons to the life
of promise; he also binds them to the continuities
of the past as he instructs them to bury him at
Machpelah, purchased by Abraham. The past and
the future are always connected in the life of faith.

What burial place is significant in your personal history?

PRAYER: Almighty God, I think ahead to my own
death, the time when I leave earthly responsibilities. Show me how to live now so that when that
time comes I will be able to leave with a blessing
on my lips. *Amen.*

"Bury My Father"

READ Genesis 50:1–14

"Now therefore let me go up, so that I may
bury my father; then I will return."

Genesis 50:5b

The riches and obvious importance of Egypt do
not turn the heads of Joseph and his brothers
from the centrality of the covenant. Egypt honors
Jacob but it cannot keep him. The elaborate ceremonial of the empire is a great tribute, but his
burial will be in Abraham's cave, not Pharaoh's
pyramid.

How would you sum up Jacob's life?

PRAYER: "The strife is o'er, the battle done; the vic-
tory of life is won; the song of triumph has begun.
Alleluia!" (Palestrina, "The Strife Is O'er, the Battle
Done," in *The Hymnbook*, p. 203). *Amen*

"God Intended It for Good"

READ Genesis 50:15–26

"Even though you intended to do harm to
me, God intended it for good, in order
to preserve a numerous people, as he is
doing today."

Genesis 50:20

Verse 20 summarizes the Joseph story: the jeopardy we experience in life is developed by God into a good salvation. Evil intentions can bring human suffering but they cannot thwart God's providence.

Compare this with Romans 8:28.

PRAYER: Merciful God, I thank you that grace is present in every circumstance, salvation being worked out in every event. I thank you for the plot of promise in which I find myself, and for the completions that I see in Jesus Christ. *Amen.*

"To Egypt with Jacob"

These are the names of the sons of Israel
who came to Egypt with Jacob, each
with his household.

Exodus 1:1

Genesis told the story of a few individuals pioneer-
ing the life of faith. Exodus tells the story of these
people becoming a nation—a faith community.

Who are the great names of Genesis?

PRAYER: Father, as I immerse myself in this story
of your people, help me to understand it as the
story of my people, understanding what it means
to be a people of God still today. *Amen.*

"Shiphrah and Puah"

READ Exodus 1:8–22

The king of Egypt said to the Hebrew
    midwives, one of whom was named
    Shiphrah and the other Puah, "When
    you act as midwives to the Hebrew
    women, and see them on the birthstool,
    if it is a boy, kill him; but if it is a girl,
    she shall live."

Exodus 1:15–16

The Egyptians got it exactly backwards: the Hebrew prosperity that they suppressed out of fear
was there to bless them. It is always amusing to
see the powerful proud defeated by the ingenuity
of the little people. The murderous command of
the king of Egypt is confounded by the earthy wit
of the Hebrew midwives.

What contrasts do you note in this story?

PRAYER: I thank you, God, for those people whose
names never get into the history books but who
make history, people whom no one ever inter-
views or celebrates but whose daily courage
makes life possible for so many. Amen.

JUNE 12

"A Fine Baby"

READ Exodus 2:1–9

The woman conceived and bore a son; and
when she saw that he was a fine baby,
she hid him three months.

Exodus 2:2

The comic theme continues: the malign official
policy is cleverly subverted into an act of rescue
and nurturing. A hostile government pays a Hebrew mother to nurse her own baby. The mean
Egyptians are tricked into kindness despite themselves!

How do you imagine the conversation of the
mother, father, and sister went that day?

PRAYER: Many times, Lord, the best intentions
turn out badly; but there must be just as many
times when bad intentions are co-opted for good
and some Pharaoh's daughter inadvertently serves
salvation. All praise! *Amen.*

"Saw Their Forced Labor"

READ Exodus 2:10–12

One day, after Moses had grown up, he
    went out to his people and saw their
    forced labor. He saw an Egyptian beating
    a Hebrew, one of his kinsfolk.

Exodus 2:11

Moses was reared in a royal Egyptian house. His
language was Egyptian, as were his education and
culture. But his heart was Hebrew. His deep iden-
tification with the oppressed people meant more
than the benefits of being in the rich and ruling
family.

Do you think Moses struggled to resolve his
Egyptian-Hebrew identity?

PRAYER: Who am I, Lord? A child of this age or of
eternity? Shaped by my culture or formed in the
image of God? You have made it clear in Christ
who I am; keep me sure of it and obedient to it.
Amen.

"Sought to Kill Moses"

READ Exodus 2:13–15a

When Pharaoh heard of it, he sought to kill
   Moses.

Exodus 2:15a

Moses is in danger a second time. He survived a
near-certain death in infancy; now as an adult he
is sentenced to be executed. People engaged in the
life of faith are familiar with the brink of death
and recognize the God who knows his way out of
the grave.

There is a lot unsaid here; imagine some of it.

PRAYER: Lord Jesus Christ, I see the willingness
with which my ancestors faced danger and death
in order to be faithful to you. Keep me from easy
compromise and smooth excuses in my discipleship; in the strong name of Jesus. Amen.

"Gershom/Alien"

READ Exodus 1:15b–22

She bore a son, and he named him
  Gershom; for he said, "I have been an
alien residing in a foreign land."

Exodus 2:22

There is poignancy in the naming of Moses' son: "Gershom" means "alien." Moses is homesick. For what? Egyptian oppression? He is much safer in Midian, but his heart is with the poor and oppressed.

Where is your true home?

PRAYER: In spite of the comforts and the securities that I experience in this world, Lord, I don't feel at home unless I am sharing your work, with your people. Thank you for being with me here and giving me a taste of wholeness in this "foreign" land. *Amen.*

JUNE 16

"God Heard Their Groaning"
READ Exodus 2:23–25

God heard their groaning, and God
   remembered his covenant with
   Abraham, Isaac, and Jacob.

                                   Exodus 2:24

Political events (the king's death) and human experience (the people's bondage) trigger profound
spiritual movements. The decisive verbs in this
passage are those for which God is the subject.
   How many God-connected verbs are here?

PRAYER: Use this story, God, to keep me in touch
with what you are doing in the world still; with
the significance of your hearing, remembering,
seeing, and knowing. Train me in daily expectations based on your involvement in every part of
history and life. *Amen.*

"Holy Ground"

READ Exodus 3:1–9

Then he said, "Come no closer! Remove the
sandals from your feet, for the place on
which you are standing is holy ground."

Exodus 3:5

From being an Egyptian prince, Moses was re-
duced to a lowly shepherd. From being at home
in a palace, he was exiled to a foreign wilderness.
At this low point he found himself on holy
ground, before God. A great act of deliverance is
being prepared. It begins in the mind and heart of
God, not in the strategy of politician or reformer.
What is the significance of the burning bush?

PRAYER: I am always trying to manufacture the
right atmosphere for meeting you, Holy God—
preparing the right setting, getting into the right
mood. Then I am surprised by your presence in
the place I least expect it, at a most unlikely time.
Create holy ground under my feet today. Amen.

"Who Am I?"

READ Exodus 3:10–12

But Moses said to God, "Who am I that I
should go to Pharaoh, and bring the
Israelites out of Egypt?"

Exodus 3:11

Moses tries to get out of God's command by
pleading inadequacy. It continues to be one of our
most popular forms of refusal. The combination
of honesty (we are, in fact, inadequate) and humility seems unanswerable. God responds not with
an argument, but with his promised presence.

What is your favorite excuse?

PRAYER: Father, instead of always looking for ways
to get out of doing your will, I want to develop a
mind-set that looks for ways to get in on it, confident that whenever you command you also provide grace and strength. *Amen.*

"What Is His Name?"

READ Exodus 3:13–17

> But Moses said to God, "If I come to the
> Israelites and say to them, 'The God of
> your ancestors has sent me to you,' and
> they ask me, 'What is his name?' what
> shall I say to them?"

Exodus 3:13

A breakthrough event: God is being, the one who
is and who brings into being all that is. God is not
simply a name for something we don't quite understand, or for a power we hope to enlist in our
aid. God is present being, I AM.

Why is a name so important?

PRAYER: Lord God Almighty, give me an understanding that will allow me to respond to your
wholeness as you are, not as I want you to be, and
to love you in your reality, not through the filter
of my fantasies, even as you continue to reveal
yourself to me in Jesus Christ. *Amen.*

JUNE 20

"Not Go Empty-Handed"

Exodus 3:18–22

"I will bring this people into such favor
with the Egyptians that, when you go,
you will not go empty-handed. . . ."

Exodus 3:21

Salvation is not bare survival by the "skin of our teeth." It is not an escape-hatch provision. The Hebrews are prepared to participate in something extravagant and festive.

In what ways are you enriched by salvation?

PRAYER: I remember Mary's prayer, Lord, and make it my own: "He has scattered the proud in the thoughts of their hearts . . . and lifted up the lowly; he has filled the hungry with good things" (Luke 1:51–53). Thank you. *Amen.*

JUNE 21

"I Have Never Been Eloquent"

READ Exodus 4:1–12

But Moses said to the LORD, "O my Lord, I
have never been eloquent, neither in the
past nor even now that you have spoken
to your servant; but I am slow of speech
and slow of tongue."

Exodus 4:10

No inadequacy in us disqualifies us from what
God commands. We are not chosen because of
who we are or what we can do, but because of
what God knows he can do through us. We are unfinished creatures, whom God wills to complete.

What are you not good at?

PRAYER: Expose my excuse-making, God, for what
it is: disguised disobedience. Make me more aware
of what you can do through me than of what I
can't do for you. Prepare me for a life of obedient
willingness in Jesus Christ. *Amen.*

JUNE 22

"Send Someone Else"

READ Exodus 4:13–17

But he said, "O my LORD, please send
someone else."

Exodus 4:13

Obedience is our most difficult act. Moses wriggles and squirms—anything but obedience! God patiently accommodates his command to every difficulty Moses raises, but the command he will not withdraw. His call is insistent and relentless.

What are some of your excuses?

PRAYER: In the end, Lord, I am grateful that you do not give up on me, don't accept my excuse-making. Even as you patiently address me with your commands, give me the patient endurance for obedience. *Amen.*

"Let Me Go Back"

READ Exodus 4:18–20

Moses went back to his father-in-law Jethro
    and said to him, "Please let me go back
    to my kindred in Egypt and see whether
    they are still living." And Jethro said to
    Moses, "Go in peace."

Exodus 4:18

Obedience not only involves willingness, it requires community. When Moses' will is finally
pliant to God's purposes, he must enlist the coop-
eration of the others in his life: father-in-law,
wife, and sons. Our obedience necessarily involves
others. "We do not live to ourselves, and we do
not die to ourselves."

Comment on Romans 14:7 in relation to Moses.

PRAYER: Just when I get to the point of saying Yes
to you, God, I find that the others aren't with me.
Show me how to be as patient with them as you
are with me: patient in my prayers, loving in my
waiting. *Amen.*

"I Will Harden His Heart"

And the LORD said to Moses, "When you
go back to Egypt, see that you perform
before Pharaoh all the wonders that I
have put in your power; but I will
harden his heart, so that he will not let
the people go."

Exodus 4:21

In this work of redemption there are things beyond
understanding in both directions: the Mosaic
miracles that show God's power, the Pharaonic
unbelief that opposes it. The willing (finally) heart
of Moses and the hardened heart of Pharaoh are
about to meet.

What difficulties has God prepared you to expect?

PRAYER: Almighty God, I often look for your presence only in the things that go my way, but you
are just as much present in people and events that
don't go my way. Like Moses, I need a lot of teaching and reminding in this area. Teach me; remind
me. *Amen.*

"Bridegroom of Blood"

READ Exodus 4:24–26

But Zipporah took a flint and cut off her
son's foreskin, and touched Moses' feet
with it, and said, "Truly you are a
bridegroom of blood to me!"

Exodus 4:25

This strange, difficult-to-interpret story at the
least tells us that the life of obedient faith and the
great work of redemption involve us in realities
beyond us: matters of hurt and suffering, matters
of life and death, of which circumcision (a healed
wound) provides the symbol.

What don't you understand about salvation?

PRAYER: Of all the things that I don't understand,
Savior God, suffering—the prevalence of it, the
seeming necessity for it—is what I understand
least. I ask for grace to embrace and receive what
you give, in the name of Christ who suffered and
died for me. *Amen.*

"The People Believed . . . and Worshiped"
READ Exodus 4:27–31

The people believed; and when they
heard that the LORD had given heed
to the Israelites and that he had seen
their misery, they bowed down and
worshiped.

Exodus 4:31

Salvation is not going to be imposed on this people; and rescue is not going to be apart from God.
The people show that they understand this and
begin to live the free life by engaging in the basic
acts of freedom: belief and worship.

What is the freest thing that you do?

PRAYER: I want to be free without engaging in the
disciplines of freedom. Return me to the beginning, not skipping anything essential along the
way, as I believe and worship my way with your
people into your salvation. *Amen.*

"I Do Not Know the Lord"

But Pharaoh said, "Who is the LORD, that I
should heed him and let Israel go? I do
not know the LORD, and I will not let
Israel go."

Exodus 5:2

Moses knows God; Pharaoh does not know God.
The story develops from that contrast. Every life
story develops out of either knowing or not knowing the Lord.

Why didn't Pharaoh know the Lord?

PRAYER: Thank you, O God, for clearly revealing
yourself in the person of Jesus Christ. And now I
am "without excuse." So I will make no more excuses, but return daily and know again what you
are showing me in my Savior. *Amen.*

"They Are Lazy"

READ Exodus 5:5–14

"But you shall require of them the same
quantity of bricks as they have made
previously; do not diminish it, for they
are lazy; that is why they cry, 'Let us go
and offer sacrifice to our God.'"

Exodus 5:8

The world's attitude to faith doesn't change: what
can't be seen can't be true. Worship is laziness.
Prayer is escapism. But we can hardly expect understanding and encouragement from people
whose only criteria for reality are size and price.

What difficulties do you encounter in society
when you worship?

PRAYER: It is maddening to be told that I am irre-
sponsible and accused of shirking when I am
doing the best of which I am capable, praising
and glorifying your name, great God. But no one
promised that these things would be easy or popular. Keep me faithful in worship. Amen.

"Why Have You Mistreated This People?"

READ Exodus 5:15–23

Then Moses turned again to the LORD and
said, "O LORD, why have you mistreated
this people? Why did you ever send me?"

Exodus 5:22

There are moments in the story of salvation that
are absolutely baffling. Instead of getting better,
everything seems to get worse. How does it happen that obedience to God's command involves us
in such difficulties?

What in your life seems worse because of your
faith?

PRAYER: I know the whole story of Israel, Father,
and so know that there will be a triumph. But I
don't know the whole story of my life and am
often bewildered in a desert darkness. At such
times create hope in me, in the name of Jesus.
Amen.

JUNE 30

"How Then Shall Pharaoh Listen?"

READ Exodus 6:1–13

> But Moses spoke to the LORD, "The
> Israelites have not listened to me; how
> then shall Pharaoh listen to me, poor
> speaker that I am?"
>
> Exodus 6:12

The objection is logical; but the work is *theological*.
If Moses can't convince his own people, it stands
to reason that he won't be able to convince
Pharaoh. But logic is not all. Salvation spills over
the confines of reason.

Do you have logical objections to God's charge
to you?

PRAYER: Almighty God, deepen my capacity for
response and obedience. I don't want to get rid of
or disparage my ability to think, but I don't want
to be limited by it either. *Amen.*

JULY 1

"These Are the Heads"

READ Exodus 6:14–27

These are the heads of the ancestral houses
of the Levites by their families.

Exodus 6:25b

The story is interrupted for the listing of families.
The storyteller pauses, just before the action esca-
lates, to make sure we have all the names straight
and know exactly who is included in the story.
The Bible takes great care in getting names straight.
It is careful and exact in the naming of God; it is
just as careful in naming people. There is no
gospel-in-general; God's salvation treats us in all
our personal uniqueness.

Are you in the story?

PRAYER: I thank you, Lord, that when I read these
scriptures I am not just getting information about
ancient history but am discovering something
personal about my own origins: that I am known,
and commanded, and saved by you. *Amen.*

JULY 2

"Great Acts of Judgment"
READ Exodus 6:28–7:7

"When Pharaoh does not listen to you, I
will lay my hand upon Egypt and bring
my people the Israelites, company by
company, out of the land of Egypt by
great acts of judgment."

Exodus 7:4

The difficulties have been faced, the objections accounted for; now the strategy is revealed: this is not
going to be a matter of subtle persuasion, but of
interruptive acts of judgment. We are going to see
how judgment is used to bring about salvation.

Is "judgment" negative or positive in your mind?

PRAYER: Father in heaven, give me the grace of understanding so that I may perceive your hand not
only in Israel's history but in my country's history—and believe that you are working your saving will in events in which many people see only
your absence. *Amen.*

"Aaron's Staff"

READ Exodus 7:8–13

Each one threw down his staff, and they
became snakes; but Aaron's staff
swallowed up theirs.

Exodus 7:12

We begin a series of confrontations between the
Egyptian powers that hold people in slavery and
the power of God that promises freedom. There
is a foretaste of eventual victory in the sign of
Aaron's rod.

How sure are you that God is more powerful
than "the powers"?

PRAYER: Almighty God, as I become more deeply
familiar with this old story of the fierce clash of
powers in Egypt, build my confidence and hope
in your power to achieve freedom and salvation in
triumph. Amen.

"Turned to Blood"

"Thus says the LORD, 'By this you shall
know that I am the LORD. See, with the
staff that is in my hand I will strike the
water that is in the Nile, and it shall be
turned to blood.'"

Exodus 7:17

The first plague—blood in the wrong place, in the
rivers instead of the veins—reverses the meaning
of that substance; instead of being a sign of life, it
is a sign of death. The plague interrupts the complacent routines of a nation that is out of touch
with God.

What recent interruption has called your attention to God?

PRAYER: Lord God, judge of all the earth, upset the
routines that keep me from being aware of your
presence, interfere with the arrangements that or-
ganize you out of the action, so that I can change
my ways and enter into your daily acts of salvation. Amen.

"The Frogs Came up"

READ Exodus 8:1–15

So Aaron stretched out his hand over the
waters of Egypt; and the frogs came up
and covered the land of Egypt.

Exodus 8:6

Second plague: frogs in the wrong place, in the
houses and food bowls instead of the swamps and
rivers. And why? Because God's people were in
the wrong place, in Egyptian slavery instead of
promised-land freedom.

What is the right place for you? Are you in it?

PRAYER: God Almighty, what will you do today to
show me the skewed nature of this sinful world
that I live in, and warn me from being conformed
to it? I don't want to miss a single sign of your
judgment. Amen.

"The Finger of God"

READ Exodus 8:16–19

And the magicians said to Pharaoh, "This is
the finger of God!" But Pharaoh's heart
was hardened, and he would not listen
to them, just as the LORD had said.

Exodus 8:19

Third plague: the intensity increases—for the first
time the magicians are out of their depth; they
cannot duplicate the feat. Pharaoh realizes that
this is not an extraordinary *man* he is dealing with
but an extraordinary *God.*

What does "finger of God" mean?

PRAYER: Am I, Lord, as thickheaded and as hard-
hearted as Pharaoh? Am I stubborn in my self-
will? Train me in quick responsiveness to your
hand in my life, and in a sustained obedience.
Amen.

"Great Swarms of Flies"

READ Exodus 8:20–24

The LORD did so, and great swarms of flies
came into the house of Pharaoh and into
his officials' houses; in all of Egypt the
land was ruined because of the flies.

Exodus 8:24

Fourth plague: this time the Israelites are exempted
from the conditions. This is yet another detail to
force a recognition that far more is going on here
than magical arts or natural disasters: God is "Lord
in the midst of the earth" (v. 22)!

Do you know where Goshen is?

PRAYER: Sometimes I find myself in the middle of
the disaster, O God, and sometimes I find myself
quite outside it. Grant me the maturity to see your
hand in all of it and my place in all of it, rather
than to evaluate your presence in terms of my
comfort level. *Amen.*

JULY 8

"Three Days' Journey"

READ Exodus 8:25–32

"We must go a three days' journey into the
wilderness and sacrifice to the LORD our
God as he commands us."

Exodus 8:27

Is Pharaoh weakening a little? Moses and Pharaoh
are like two men haggling in the marketplace,
back and forth, probing for a weakness, looking
for an advantage. An opening appears: the discussion is not *whether* they will go, but *how far*. Pharaoh
is being "softened" toward obedience.

Are you good at putting off obedience?

PRAYER: I look over the years of my pilgrimage,
Lord, and realize how patient you have been with
me, but at the same time how insistent. You do
not let me go! Thank you for keeping after me
and staying with me. *Amen.*

"A Distinction Between the Livestock"

READ Exodus 9:1–7

"But the LORD will make a distinction
between the livestock of Israel and the
livestock of Egypt, so that nothing shall
die of all that belongs to the Israelites."

Exodus 9:4

Fifth plague: with this plague, judgment moves
into the realm of property. When we think more
of possessions than of God, the only way God can
get our attention is through loss of possessions.

What possessions mean the most to you?

PRAYER: I praise you for the material world of animals and things. Help me to receive your gifts
rightly, and never let them substitute for your will
or presence in my life. *Amen.*

"Festering Boils"

READ Exodus 9:8–12

So they took soot from the kiln, and stood
before Pharaoh, and Moses threw it in
the air, and it caused festering boils on
humans and animals.

Exodus 9:10

Sixth plague: this is the first of the plagues to
touch the person. The others have caused immense inconvenience and loss of property; this
one introduces personal pain. God sometimes
uses illness or pain to get our attention.

Has any occasion of sickness brought you
closer to God?

PRAYER: I know you are the Great Physician, Lord;
and I look to you for healing. Help me also to be
ready to see your hand in my illnesses, my body
telling me that I am living in disobedience or in
faithlessness. *Amen.*

"Such Heavy Hail"

READ Exodus 9:13–26

. . . there was hail with fire flashing
continually in the midst of it, such heavy
hail as had never fallen in all the land of
Egypt since it became a nation.

Exodus 9:24

Seventh plague: the special feature here is that this
plague's consequences can be escaped by taking
shelter—a field trip in experiencing the practical
results of doing what God says. The point of these
plagues is not to destroy people but to get them to
obey God's word.

What difference does obedience make in your
life?

PRAYER: Father in heaven, I want to be especially
attentive through the hours of this day to the ways
your word shapes my life, enters into my everyday
actions, forms my attitudes and speech—for good
and not for evil. Amen.

"You Do Not Yet Fear"

READ Exodus 9:27–35

"But as for you and your officials, I know
that you do not yet fear the LORD God."

Exodus 9:30

Moses had enough experience now to be skeptical: Pharaoh was looking for a way out of judgment, not into obedience. All that energy and intelligence were being used to avoid God, when he could have been embracing salvation!

Is there anything like this in your life?

PRAYER: Gracious and merciful Lord, I should be used to the persistence of sin and the ingenuity of unbelief, in both myself and my neighbors, but I'm not. But the persistence and ingenuity of grace are greater, and for that I praise you. Amen.

JULY 13

"No, Never!"

READ Exodus 10:1–11

"No, never! Your men may go and worship
the LORD, for that is what you are asking."

Exodus 10:11a

Against the pleas of Moses, against the advice of
his own servants, and in the midst of the ruina-
tion all around him, Pharaoh stubbornly repeats
his "no!" This is not a refusal of strength but of
weakness—the reaction of a superstitious, frightened man, suspecting "evil purpose" in the unknown.

Do you know people for whom God is always
viewed as a threat?

PRAYER: I often interpret people's rejection of you,
O God, as self-willed defiance; but maybe more
often it is terror of the unknown God. Show me
how I can share the news of a gracious God with
these people. *Amen.*

"A Dense Swarm of Locusts"

READ Exodus 10:12–20

The locusts came upon all the land of
Egypt and settled on the whole country
of Egypt, such a dense swarm of locusts
as had never been before, nor ever shall
be again.

Exodus 10:14

Eighth plague: the food supply is destroyed. Egypt
along the Nile was richly fertile; the locust plague
took away the food for the morrow. The judgment
produced a day of (involuntary) fasting. Was it
also a day of prayer for a change of heart in their
ruler?

What disasters have worked repentance in you?

PRAYER: Lord, I wonder where I am still holding
out against you. Are there secret strongholds of
rebellion in my life? Are there persistent "no's"
that I keep beneath the surface of my diplomatic
show of belief? Amen.

"A Darkness That Can Be Felt"

READ Exodus 10:21–29

Then the LORD said to Moses, "Stretch out
your hand toward heaven so that there
may be darkness over the land of Egypt,
a darkness that can be felt."

Exodus 10:21

Ninth plague: the withdrawal of light from the
creation. God's first words were "Let there be
light." The refusal to listen to God's word returns
us to the dark—blind and groping. A life without
God's word is a dark world.

Compare these three days with the three hours
of Matthew 27:45.

PRAYER: Lord of light, your words and your work
illuminate my life. I don't want to be deprived of
a single ray of your bright presence. I want to be
a child of the day every day. *Amen.*

"Objects of Silver and Gold"

READ Exodus 11:1–3

"Tell the people that every man is to ask his
neighbor and every woman is to ask her
neighbor for objects of silver and gold."

Exodus 11:2

Deep contrasts are developing in the story: while
Pharaoh is hardening his heart, the people are
softening theirs. Pharaoh holds on tightly to his
slave people; his own people open their hands in
generosity. Moses, rejected by Pharaoh, is re-
spected by Pharaoh's people and servants.

How do people respond to your Christian witness?

PRAYER: I know better than to expect it all the
time, Father, but I thank you for those occasions
when I experience support and approval from
those around me in my pursuit of righteousness.
Amen.

JULY 17

"The Firstborn"

READ Exodus 11:4–10

> "Every firstborn in the land of Egypt shall
> die, from the firstborn of Pharaoh who
> sits on his throne to the firstborn of the
> female slave who is behind the handmill,
> and all the firstborn of the livestock."
>
> Exodus 11:5

Tenth plague: the death of the firstborn. The nine
previous plagues moved from periphery to center,
tightening the grip of judgment on the jugular of
unbelief. This final plague is announced before it
is put into effect—there is still time to repent.

Have you ever experienced "hardening of the
heart"?

PRAYER: God, I look at Pharaoh's intractable stub-
bornness with amazement—how can he, in daily
direct confrontation with the work of God, persist
in undeviating unbelief? And then I think about
how slow I am to believe. Soften my heart, O
God, to your love. *Amen.*

"I Will Pass over You"

READ Exodus 12:1–13

"The blood shall be a sign for you on the houses where you live: when I see the blood, I will pass over you, and no plague shall destroy you when I strike the land of Egypt."

Exodus 12:13

As God prepares to deliver his people from bondage, he also prepares the act of worship that will keep the deliverance alive in their experience as a free people. And it has been kept alive all these centuries—the passover meal is prepared and eaten, and God is praised.

Do you think of this story when you receive holy communion?

PRAYER: I meditate, Father, on this story of my ancestors and connect it with the story of my Lord Jesus; together they are the story of my salvation. These are the stories that tell me who I am, and what you have done that makes me what I am. All praise, Father! Amen.

"You Shall Eat Unleavened Bread"

READ Exodus 12:14–20

"Seven days you shall eat unleavened bread;
  on the first day you shall remove leaven
  from your houses, for whoever eats
  leavened bread from the first day until
  the seventh day shall be cut off from
  Israel."

Exodus 12:15

Leaven in this context symbolizes the rebellious hardness of heart that characterized Egypt. The week-long elimination of leaven provides a forceful, imaginative strategy for a discerning separation of the Egyptian "leaven" from the salvation meal.

What rituals do you have that remind you of what God is doing?

PRAYER: Lord, as I practice your presence this day, keep me alert to the meaning of everything around me, as signs of your work in creation and salvation. *Amen.*

JULY 20

"Select Lambs"

READ Exodus 12:21–28

Then Moses called all the elders of Israel and
said to them, "Go, select lambs for your
families, and slaughter the passover lamb."

Exodus 12:21

Here is the origin of the powerful and pervasive
lamb imagery found in the gospel. We understand
Jesus, "the lamb of God who takes away the sin
of the world," in the context of this long-remem-
bered and much-practiced obedience and worship.

What does "lamb" bring to your remembrance?

PRAYER: "Dear dying Lamb, Thy precious blood
shall never lose its power till all the ransomed
Church of God be saved, to sin no more, be saved
to sin no more" (William Cowper, "There Is a
Fountain Filled with Blood," in *The Hymnbook*,
p. 276). *Amen.*

"Go Away"

READ Exodus 12:29–32

Then he summoned Moses and Aaron in the
night, and said, "Rise up, go away from
my people, both you and the Israelites!
Go, worship the LORD, as you said."

Exodus 12:31

Free at last. Finally, the releasing word from
Pharaoh. It took ten plagues, each more severe
than the last, to get Pharaoh to loosen his grip on
this people. The world does not easily let us go,
but in the end it must.

Are there parts of your life that are still in
"Egypt"?

PRAYER: I am learning some things about your
judgments, God. They are terrifying to people
who are rebellious, but they are freeing to people
who are obedient. Keep me among the obedient,
hoping and believing as my life is shaped by worship of my Lord and Savior. *Amen.*

"They Plundered the Egyptians"

READ Exodus 12:33–36

> . . . and the LORD had given the people
> favor in the sight of the Egyptians, so
> that they let them have what they asked.
> And so they plundered the Egyptians.
>
> Exodus 12:36

The Egyptians are left with nothing; the Israelites leave with everything. There is nothing exciting or luxurious about sin; the stories and advertisements are an enormous lie. The people who reject God end up bereft. And salvation is not poverty-stricken but gathers us into a vast plenitude.

Compare this with Exodus 3:18–22.

PRAYER: Too often, Lord Jesus, I get brainwashed by the lies of my culture and interpret my life of faith by what I give up. Use this story to show me how full of favor my life now is, and how empty that grasping life from which you delivered me. Amen.

"Could Not Wait"

READ Exodus 12:37–39

They baked unleavened cakes of the dough
    that they had brought out of Egypt; it
    was not leavened, because they were
    driven out of Egypt and could not wait,
    nor had they prepared any provisions for
    themselves.

Exodus 12:39

Here is the history behind the instructions on unleavened bread (vv. 14–20). They left in a hurry!
There was no time to let the bread rise. Salvation
must not be procrastinated; obedience must not
be compromised by dawdling. And yet they left
with everything they needed—and more (but not
everything they were used to having).

What have you left behind as you have entered
into faith?

PRAYER: Lord God, I don't want to see how much
I can take with me of my old life, or look back
with nostalgic regret at what I left behind. I want
to be quick to obey you, with good faith reflexes.
Amen.

"A Night of Vigil"

READ Exodus 12:40–42

That was for the LORD a night of vigil, to
  bring them out of the land of Egypt.
  That same night is a vigil to be kept for
  the LORD by all the Israelites throughout
  their generations.

Exodus 12:42

It was in the middle of the night, when the darkness was deepest and despair nearly total (if nine plagues had not worked, what chance did a tenth have?), that salvation took place. Still, in the night darkness in which we cannot see our way, God watches us and leads us into light.

What gospel night does this remind you of?

PRAYER: Nothing is the same anymore, Father. My experiences of darkness, of despair, of bewilderment have, by your grace, become light and hope and assurance. I thank you for the deep and lasting changes that I am living through in Christ. *Amen.*

"One Law for the Native and for the Alien"

READ Exodus 12:43–51

". . . there shall be one law for the native and
for the alien who resides among you."

Exodus 12:49

The passover must never be permitted to be a sec-
ular celebration; it is a faith celebration. No one is
excluded except those who refuse faith: provision
is made to bring everyone whom we encounter to
the meal by inviting commitment to God and response to his salvation.

Why is this instruction important?

PRAYER: God, I don't want to lower my life to the
level of the people around me who are strangers
to faith, but by my words and actions attract and
invite them to life on the highest plane. Amen.

JULY 26

"Remember"

READ Exodus 13:1–10

Moses said to the people, "Remember this
day on which you came out of Egypt, out
of the house of slavery, because the LORD
brought you out from there by strength of
hand; no leavened bread shall be eaten."

Exodus 13:3

If we have no memory we have no identity; without memory there is no continuity to our lives
and we begin each day from scratch. The deepest
memories reach back beyond what we did yesterday into what God did before we were born; they
connect us with those actions that reach into and
shape our present.

What provisions do you make for remembrance?

PRAYER: Keep the past alive in my present, Father,
so that everything I do today takes place with an
awareness of the centuries of graciousness, the
richly documented love, the ever-proven salvation
to which I am heir in Jesus Christ. *Amen.*

JULY 27

"What Does This Mean?"

READ Exodus 13:11–16

"When in the future your child asks you,
  'What does this mean?' you shall answer,
  'By strength of hand the LORD brought us
  out of Egypt, from the house of slavery.'"

Exodus 13:14

The contrast between the death of the Egyptian firstborn and the consecration of the Hebrew firstborn keeps the basic themes of judgment and salvation alive in the experience of the people. Every birth of child and animal is a trigger to activate the memory.

How many times does "firstborn" occur here?

PRAYER: God Almighty, you have placed me in the midst of birth and death, the great boundary events of my existence. Keep me attentive to these vast essentials, pondering their meaning, finding your presence in them, through Jesus Christ. *Amen.*

"The Bones of Joseph"

READ Exodus 13:17–22

And Moses took with him the bones of
Joseph who had required a solemn oath
of the Israelites, saying, "God will surely
take notice of you, and then you must
carry my bones with you from here."

Exodus 13:19

The great pilgrim journey begins. The Israelites
are venturing into the unknown, guided by God.
But it is not the first time this land has been traveled in faith; their ancestor Joseph also walked
this road. Carrying his bones with them is a way
of incorporating his story in their own.

Who are some of the important people in your
past?

PRAYER: I have the feeling often, O God, that I am
the first one to be doing this, that my doubts,
questions, trials, difficulties are unique to me.
And then I learn of others and know that there is
a fellowship in suffering, a companionship in the
congregation that knows the joyful sound. *Amen.*

JULY 29

"The Egyptians Pursued Them"

READ Exodus 14:1–18

The Egyptians pursued them, all Pharaoh's
   horses and chariots, his chariot drivers
   and his army; they overtook them
   camped by the sea, by Pi-hahiroth, in
   front of Baal-zephon.

Exodus 14:9

A great war story begins. Pharaoh's hostility reasserts itself: he assumes the Israelites are easy
prey; he mobilizes all his military prowess; he will
catch his runaway slaves. He still doesn't realize
that he is dealing with God.

When did you first hear this story?

PRAYER: There is a little bit of Pharaoh in me, O
God. The moment the pressure is off I begin trying to get my own way again. The moment things
seem normal, I rush headlong after whatever I
think will make me happy. When will I ever learn?
Amen.

JULY 30

"The Pillar of Cloud"

READ Exodus 14:19–20

The angel of God who was going before
the Israelite army moved and went
behind them; and the pillar of cloud
moved from in front of them and took
its place behind them.

Exodus 14:19

The cloud is both light and darkness. Collecting
the rays of sun and moon, it is full of light. But it
is also opaque, preventing us from seeing through
it. On that night (and every night), God was
surely present and deeply mysterious. We know
that he will save us; we don't know how he will
save us.

Have you ever had nights like this?

PRAYER: Almighty God, I thank you for the many
times that I have been assured of your presence.
Through nights of uncertainty I have come to
know your salvation, and have awakened to a new
day unharmed and whole. Amen.

"The Waters Were Divided"

READ Exodus 14:21–25

> Then Moses stretched out his hand over the sea. The LORD drove the sea back by a strong east wind all night, and turned the sea into dry land; and the waters were divided.
>
> Exodus 14:21

The sea that appeared to be an impenetrable barrier opened up as the way of escape. What the Israelites had seen as the place of their death became a gate of salvation. Our gloomy (or cocky) convictions are turned upside down by God's action.

When have you been surprised by God?

PRAYER: Lord God of Hosts, I look at the world, calculate my chances, and know that I can never make it. Then I see your hand in my life, discover your grace in my heart, and know that my worst fears are over and your will is done. *Amen.*

"Israel Saw the Great Work"

READ Exodus 14:26–31

Israel saw the great work that the LORD
did against the Egyptians. So the people
feared the LORD and believed in the
LORD and in his servant Moses.

Exodus 14:31

The great work is salvation. The Israelites had
feared the visible Pharaoh and believed his power
was supreme; now they feared the invisible God
and let his power shape their lives. This day was
pivotal in the life of Israel, and remains pivotal for
every person of faith.

How is this day similar to the day of Jesus'
resurrection?

PRAYER: Gracious and powerful God, I know that
salvation is the great work, and there is none
greater, but I slip into lesser things, and am entangled in trivial pursuits. Return me to this pivot
where you are shaping my life for eternity,
through Jesus Christ my risen Lord. Amen.

AUGUST 2

"Sang This Song"

READ Exodus 15:1–12

Then Moses and the Israelites sang this
   song to the LORD:
"I will sing to the LORD, for he has
   triumphed gloriously;
horse and rider he has thrown into
   the sea."

Exodus 15:1

Chapter 14 tells the story of the exodus; chapter
15 sings it. The story requires expression both
ways, in sober narration and in ecstatic song.
Every part of our faith has to be both said and
sung. The exodus experience was not remembered as a contest between Egyptian and Israelite
but as the incomparable action of God. God enters
history! He is not a comforting background to
human affairs, but the front-and-center action.
   What images in this song impress you most?

PRAYER: Almighty God, I want to sing a song like
this about my life, a song that celebrates you as
the one who is at the very center of the action, the
one without whom nothing can be understood,
the one by whom everything is celebrated. *Amen.*

"You Brought Them in"
READ Exodus 15:13–21

When the horses of Pharoah with his chariots
and his chariot drivers went into the sea,
the LORD brought back the waters of the
sea upon them; but the Israelites walked
through the sea on dry ground.

Exodus 15:19

Nothing that the Israelites will face in the days
ahead can be any worse than what they have just
been through. What God has done, he will do.
Salvation is not only an event to be remembered,
it is the reality that continues until God's will is
completed.

What do you no longer fear because of God's
salvation?

PRAYER: Dear God, I want to be as hopeful for the
future as I am grateful for the past. I want everything I have experienced and believed to carry me
full of courage and obedience into the days ahead.
Amen.

"Marah"

READ Exodus 15:22–27

When they came to Marah, they could not
  drink the water of Marah because it was
  bitter. That is why it was called Marah.

Exodus 15:23

The triumphant song of salvation is followed by a
challenge to faith. Three days into their life of salvation, the Israelites find the water undrinkable.
The song of salvation modulates into a murmur-
ing drone; the life of blessing turns bitter. Will
they become bitter? God shows himself able to
sustain in the everyday necessities as well as in
life-threatening crises.

What are you complaining about today?

PRAYER: Why is it easier to trust you in the big
things than in the little things, Lord? I trust you
for my salvation, but murmur when I lack some
daily necessity. Help me to learn praise in the ordinary. Amen.

"Complained"

READ Exodus 16:1–3

The whole congregation of the Israelites
complained against Moses and Aaron in
the wilderness.

Exodus 16:2

By and large, people prefer a comfortable slavery
to an arduous freedom. In *The City of God*, Augustine observed that the people around him were
"more pained if their villa is poor than if their life
is bad." Before we appreciate the glories of a free
life in Christ, we are very apt to complain of its
austerities.

What is the most difficult thing for you in
being free?

PRAYER: Forgive my much complaining, Lord.
Help me to enter into this extraordinary life of
freedom in Christ and discover and appreciate all
the dimensions of its glory. *Amen.*

AUGUST 6

"He Has Heard Your Complaining"

READ Exodus 16:4–12

". . . and in the morning you shall see the
glory of the LORD, because he has heard
your complaining against the LORD. For
what are we, that you complain against us?"

Exodus 16:7

Even our complainings are accepted as acts of
prayer by a gracious God. This is prayer at its min-
imal—mean, carping, ungrateful—and yet prayer
it is, for God listens and responds. The merest
groan is a seed prayer.

Are you surprised at God's amazing grace?

PRAYER: My praying, Lord, is a pretty sorry per-
formance: a litany of complaint and criticism.
And your response is an amazing grace: listening
to me in my ugliness, working with me in my
twisted self-seeking, showing me your glory in
the wilderness. *Amen.*

"As Much as Each Needed"

READ Exodus 16:13–21

But when they measured it with an omer,
those who gathered much had nothing
over, and those who gathered little had
no shortage; they gathered as much as
each of them needed.

Exodus 16:18

Quail in the evening, bread in the morning: God's children are being trained in the difficult discipline of *enough*. Not too much, not too little, but enough. But some, not trusting God to be as gracious tomorrow as he is today, hoarded. God gives according to our need, not according to our greed.

Is "enough" enough for you?

PRAYER: "I look to Thee in every need, and never look in vain; I feel Thy strong and tender love, and all is well again; the thought of Thee is mightier far than sin and pain and sorrow are" (Samuel Longfellow, "I Look to Thee in Every Need," in *The Hymnbook*, p. 114). *Amen.*

"Two Omers Apiece"
READ Exodus 16:22–30

> On the sixth day they gathered twice as
> much food, two omers apiece.
>
> Exodus 16:22a

In the midst of providing for the Israelites' physical survival, God gives the sabbath for spiritual survival, and establishes its priority by arranging the bread-gathering to support the sabbath-keeping, and not the other way around.

How committed are you to keeping the sabbath?

PRAYER: Father in heaven, I relish my daily bread and receive it with gratitude. Help me to be as enthusiastic and grateful in my weekly worship. *Amen.*

"Ate Manna Forty Years"

READ Exodus 16:31–36

The Israelites ate manna forty years, until
they came to a habitable land; they ate
manna, until they came to the border of
the land of Canaan.

Exodus 16:35

A jug of manna doesn't look like much when set
alongside a dazzling creation visible in ocean deeps
and mountain heights, or in comparison with a
stunning redemption remembered in the song of
Moses and the passover ritual. But, in fact, it is no
less a marvel—"daily bread" for forty years!

How do you continue thankful for the daily
blessings?

PRAYER: Faithful Father, thank you for air to
breathe and food to eat, a sun that shines and
water to drink—this amazing life-giving world
that I awake to and enter each morning! *Amen.*

"Massah and Meribah"

READ Exodus 17:1–7

He called the place Massah and Meribah,
because the Israelites quarreled and
tested the LORD, saying, "Is the LORD
among us or not?"

Exodus 17:7

We wonder how God would have provided for his people if they had not complained. We will never know, but we can be sure that a trusting people would have experienced our Lord's providence in quite different ways than this contentious people did.

Read Psalm 95.

PRAYER: When I experience times of need, O Lord, it is the easiest thing in the world to fill the air with complaints. How much I must miss of grace by my whining beggary. I'd like to learn to express trust and let you surprise me with your gifts. Amen.

"Held up His Hands"

> But Moses' hands grew weary; so they took
> a stone and put it under him, and he sat
> on it. Aaron and Hur held up his hands,
> one on one side, and the other on the
> other side; so his hands were steady
> until the sun set.

> Exodus 17:12

The great Moses couldn't do it alone; he needed help. Aaron and Hur, holding up his hands that day, were as essential to victory as Moses, whose hands directed and blessed.

Whose help are you dependent upon these days?

PRAYER: "O brother man, fold to thy heart thy brother; where pity dwells, the peace of God is there; to worship rightly is to love each other, each smile a hymn, each kindly deed a prayer" (John Greenleaf Whittier, "O Brother Man," in *The Hymnbook*, p. 474). *Amen.*

"Jethro"

READ Exodus 18:1–9

> Jethro, the priest of Midian, Moses' father-in-law, heard of all that God had done for Moses and for his people Israel, how the LORD had brought Israel out of Egypt.
>
> Exodus 18:1

This touching scene of reunion with wife, sons, and father-in-law is one of the rare glimpses we get of Moses' family life. The reunion seems to have gone much the way ours do—catching up on what has happened since we last saw each other, and rejoicing that everything has gone so well.

Notice the contrast with the last mention of Zipporah in Exodus 4:24–26.

PRAYER: Keep my feet on the ground, Lord, and close to the people to whom I am parent and spouse and child. I want to share the great things you do with the persons who are closest to me. *Amen.*

"Now I Know"

READ Exodus 18:10–12

"Now I know that the LORD is greater than
all gods, because he delivered the people
from the Egyptians, when they dealt
arrogantly with them."

Exodus 18:11

The story of deliverance that Moses tells brings his
father-in-law to a confession of faith. Stories, not
arguments, continue to be the norm by which
most people are brought to belief.

How do you witness—with stories or with arguments?

PRAYER: What a great story I am in on, O God!
Such a story of grace and deliverance. Help me to
be quick and skillful in passing the story on to
others, so that it also becomes their story. Amen.

"Why Do You Sit Alone?"

READ Exodus 18:13–23

> When Moses' father-in-law saw all that
> he was doing for the people, he said,
> "What is this that you are doing for the
> people? Why do you sit alone, while all
> the people stand around you from
> morning until evening?"
>
> Exodus 18:14

Why was Moses trying to do everything by himself? Jethro taught him how to share responsibility and delegate authority. Although only a day old in the faith, Jethro was mature with a commonsense wisdom that the Red Sea veteran lacked.

What unexpected "outsider" has given you wise counsel?

PRAYER: God of truth and wisdom, bring the right people into my life, people who can instruct me in living well, in grafting into the life of salvation a life of mature wisdom. In Jesus' name. *Amen.*

"Moses Chose Able Men"

Moses chose able men from all Israel
   and appointed them as heads over the
   people. . . .

Exodus 18:25a

What could his sheepherding father-in-law teach the accomplished and Egyptian-educated Moses about government and administration? Besides he was a mere newcomer to the faith. But Moses in humility accepted his counsel and in the process became wise.

Who are some of your helpers?

PRAYER: I thank you for the great company of people among whom you have placed me, Lord, and for the ways you are teaching us to share ministries of helping and serving one another. Keep me faithful in my part and thankful for their parts. Amen.

"A Priestly Kingdom"

READ Exodus 19:1–9

". . . but you shall be for me a priestly
kingdom and a holy nation. These are
the words that you shall speak to the
Israelites."

Exodus 19:6

A priest presents a person's needs before God,
presents God to the person in need. In Egypt
priests were a privileged class, lording it over
common folk. In Israel the people are to do this
for one another.

To whom are you a priest?

PRAYER: It is difficult to realize the true identity,
great God, of these friends around me—priests
presenting you to me! Help me to be a good and
faithful priest to those I meet today. *Amen.*

"Consecrate Them"

READ Exodus 19:10–15

. . . the LORD said to Moses: "Go to the people
and consecrate them today and tomorrow.
Have them wash their clothes. . . ."

Exodus 19:10

This priesthood into which they are all being initiated requires the most careful preparation. From
now on, life is no longer a matter of dealing with
the world, but primarily with God. Each of them
(each of us!) is "set apart from all common uses
to this holy use and mystery" (The Book of Common
Worship, 1946, p. 161).

How are you "set apart"?

PRAYER: When I let other people define my life,
Father, I regard myself in terms of what I can do
that pays off, what I contribute to the economy.
When I let you define my life, I realize who I am,
and how sacred and precious every part of my life
is. Amen.

"God Would Answer Him in Thunder"

READ Exodus 19:16–25

As the blast of the trumpet grew louder
and louder, Moses would speak and God
would answer him in thunder.

Exodus 19:19

Nothing is more awesome than the word of God.
Are we too jaded to be in awe? In a world filled
with bibles and sermons, we lose awareness of
this grand and life-centering fact: that God should
speak to us! that we should hear God!

How is your life changed by God's word?

PRAYER: Let me hear it afresh, in thunder,
Almighty God—the word that makes me whole,
that shapes my salvation, that gives me direction,
that declares my destiny, that brings me love;
through Jesus Christ my Lord, the word made
flesh. Amen.

"Idol"

READ *Exodus 20:4–6*

"You shall not make for yourself an idol,
   whether in the form of anything that is
   in heaven above, or that is on the earth
   beneath, or that is in the water under
   the earth."

Exodus 20:4

How do we keep the fact of the invisible God before us? Why not an image? But the image, reminding, also reduces: the god is under my control, dependent upon my care. If I am going to keep God before me, it is going to have to be by faith, not by fabrication.

Can you think of further reasons that idol-making is forbidden?

PRAYER: Lord, I am always trying to make things easier than they are; and having a visible god would certainly be easier! But it is truth that I finally want, not convenience. Train me in the life of faith in which the "things not seen" (Hebrews 11:3) are as real, and finally more real than the things seen. *Amen.*

"All These Words"

READ *Exodus 20:1*

Then God spoke all these words. . . .

Exodus 20:1

"These words" are among the most familiar in scripture, and absolutely definitive for understanding our existence. This is the way the world works. The commandments describe the "grain" of the universe. And if you go against the grain, you get splinters.

Have you memorized the Ten Commandments?

PRAYER: Thank you, gracious and almighty God, for putting it all down in black and white so that I don't have to guess my way, finding out by trial and error what works and what doesn't. *Amen.*

AUGUST 20

"Brought You out"

READ Exodus 20:2

"I am the LORD your God, who brought
you out of the land of Egypt, out of the
house of slavery. . . ."

Exodus 20:2

Before the ten imperatives, there is one grand in-
dicative. Before we are commanded, we are saved.
We often get it backwards, thinking that keeping
the commandments finally adds up to our salvation. The reality is that God's act of salvation is the
ground and source of our obedience.

Do you ever get it backwards?

PRAYER: Help me to keep the proportions right, O
God. Help me to understand that the great, massive, overwhelming reality is the salvation that
you wrought for me, and that any obedience I
manage is because of and in response to that.
Amen.

AUGUST 21

"No Other Gods"

READ Exodus 20:3

". . . you shall have no other gods before me."

Exodus 20:3

God is one. "Other gods," therefore, are not gods
at all but illusions or fabrications or falsifications.
Insofar as we "have" them we give ourselves over
to unreality, diminish our hold on life, and waste-
fully adulterate our precious humanness, which
comes to expression in faith and worship.

What "other gods" have you deliberately se
aside?

PRAYER: God Almighty, I have no trouble believi
that you and only you are God, but I do have tr
ble living single-mindedly before you. I am
vulnerable to distractions, such an easy pre
seductions. "Give me an undivided heart to r
your name" (Psalm 86:11). Amen.

"The Name"

READ Exodus 20:7

"You shall not make wrongful use of the
name of the LORD your God, for the
LORD will not acquit anyone who
misuses his name."

Exodus 20:7

We do not have a god-in-general, a kind of divinity-
in-abstraction, but a God revealed, the Lord, who
tells us his will, who enters into relation with us.
It is empty and vain to gossip *about* God, referring
to him in a name-dropping way. It is serious and
proper to speak *to* him, personally and reverently.
    Do you mostly talk *about* God or *to* him?

PRAYER: Lord God, I want prayer to be my primary
address: speaking to you and not about you,
bringing myself attentively before you just as you
have brought yourself sacrificially before me in
Jesus Christ. *Amen.*

AUGUST 24

"Remember the Sabbath"

READ Exodus 20:8–11

"Remember the sabbath day, and keep it holy."

Exodus 20:8

"Sabbath" means quit, stop, take a break. Spend the day not doing so that you become aware of God, his will, and his glory. Our work is not the most important thing. Sabbath interrupts us in the midst of unfinished work and insists that we attend for a while to God's finished work.

How do you observe the sabbath?

PRAYER: Merciful, gracious, and holy God, help me to keep a good sabbath this week: getting out of the way so that I can realize your way, stopping the frenzy of my activity so that I can see and appreciate your great work, being quiet long enough to hear your still, small voice. *Amen.*

"Honor"

READ Exodus 20:12

"Honor your father and your mother, so
    that your days may be long in the land
    that the LORD your God is giving you."

Exodus 20:12

Powerful forces of self-will are a constant threat to
family stability. The strong command to honor
parents counters this self-will and provides the
conditions in which love can be learned, wisdom
transmitted, and intimacy realized.

Think of some details of what "honor" involves.

PRAYER: Father in heaven, as I receive the life and
love that you give me, help me to practice this life
and love with my parents; and, as I am a parent, to
pass them on to my children. *Amen*

AUGUST 26

"Murder"

"You shall not murder."

Exodus 20:13

Why is murder so common? When another interferes with my happiness, or my will, I have to
decide which is more important: the inviolable
integrity of that life or the immediate gratification
of my will. The command forbids getting my way
at the expense of another's life—whether by
physical murder or verbal put-down.

Ponder Jesus' comment in Matthew 5:21–26.

PRAYER: By your command, O God, I want to
meet each person today, not as an interruption in
my plans or an obstruction to my will, but as a
never-to-be-repeated life, made in your image, in
whom I can meet the very person of Jesus Christ
(Matthew 25:40). Amen.

"Adultery"

READ Exodus 20:14

"You shall not commit adultery."

Exodus 20:14

Marriage requires our undivided attention, our uninterrupted commitment. It integrates two capacities that are often separate: ecstatic intimacy and steadfast faithfulness. The command protects this grand and difficult venture in uniting (marrying!) contraries from interference and distraction.

Why is this command so frequently violated?

PRAYER: Thank you, Father, for the gift of marriage. Thank you also for your command that guards the gift from exploitation. I pray for my married friends, that you will give them the grace of a long and faithful love. *Amen.*

AUGUST 28

"Steal"

READ Exodus 20:15

"You shall not steal."

Exodus 20:15

Things are spiritual. Material has its origin in God. The visible, tangible world is not stuff that we can plunder at will. The command insists that having learned to respect God and persons, we extend that also to things.

Do you respect the things God made as much as you do the God who made them?

PRAYER: Lord God, maker of heaven and earth, help me to see everything around me as evidence of your creative bounty and not loot to gratify my appetites. Free me from wanting to get it for myself, so that I can appreciate it in itself. *Amen.*

AUGUST 29

"False Witness"

READ Exodus 20:16

"You shall not bear false witness against
   your neighbor."

Exodus 20:16

Words are sacred, the only containers of truth that
we have. If we use them to mislead or deceive, we
violate one of our most precious realities—the
ability to communicate, the gift of communion.

Are you careful with your words?

PRAYER: I thank you, O God, for the gift of language: the ability to make myself known, and to
know. Guard my lips so that I will never use words
to diminish others or to misrepresent you. Make
all my words an accurate witness of the world that
you created and the people you love. *Amen.*

AUGUST 30

"Covet"

READ Exodus 20:17

"You shall not covet your neighbor's
house; you shall not covet your
neighbor's wife, or male or female slave,
or ox, or donkey, or anything that
belongs to your neighbor."

Exodus 20:17

The first commandment summarizes our relation
to God; the last, our relation to our neighbor. To
covet is to look to others, instead of to God, as the
source of some indispensable good. Coveting sets
us on the way to getting it out of them by any
means we can devise.

How do you deal with the impulses to covet-
ousness?

PRAYER: "I look to Thee in every need, And never
look in vain; I feel Thy strong and tender love,
And all is well again; The thought of Thee is
mightier far Than sin and pain and sorrow are"
(Samuel Longfellow, "I Look to Thee in Every
Need," in The Hymnbook, p. 114). Amen.

"So That You Do Not Sin"

READ Exodus 20:18–20

Moses said to the people, "Do not be
afraid; for God has come only to test you
and to put the fear of him upon you so
that you do not sin."

Exodus 20:20

The thunder of God's word frightened the people.
They were right to be in awe; they were wrong to
be fearful. God speaks not to destroy but to save
us. It is the thunder not of anger but of love.

Are you in awe of God's word?

PRAYER: Almighty God, speak again in thunder to
me. Catch my attention and arrest my waywardness. Command my obedience and direct my
faithfulness. *Amen.*

SEPTEMBER 1

"An Altar of Earth"

READ Exodus 20:21–26

"You need make for me only an altar of
earth and sacrifice on it your burnt
offerings and your offerings of well-
being, your sheep and your oxen; in
every place where I cause my name to be
remembered I will come to you and
bless you."

Exodus 20:24

God's words must be recalled over and over again.
The memory must not be vague but sharply affirmed in actual places, at altars. The altars must
not call attention to themselves—nothing showy
or elaborate—so that the word may remain preeminent.

Where do you best remember God's word?

PRAYER: "O God of earth and altar, Bow down and
hear our cry; Our earthly rulers falter, Our people
drift and die; The walls of gold entomb us, The
swords of scorn divide; Take not Thy thunder from
us, But take away our pride" (G. K. Chesterton, "O
God of Earth and Altar," in The Hymnbook, p. 511).
Amen.

"When"

READ Exodus 21

"These are the ordinances that you shall set
  before them: When . . ."

Exodus 21:1

Understanding the commandments is the first
step; applying them is the second. And it is not as
easy as we think. The repeated "whens" in this
chapter show the great diversity of situations in
which we work out moral solutions.

Have you ever been in any of these situations?

PRAYER: I think I understand your commands,
Lord God; but I am going to spend the rest of my
life trying to live them out in the rough-and-
tumble of emotions and relations and events. Be
with me as I do it so that your justice and mercy
will be evident in my actions. *Amen.*

SEPTEMBER 3

"If"

READ Exodus 22

"If a thief is found breaking in, and is
   beaten to death, no bloodguilt is
   incurred; but if it happens after sunrise,
   bloodguilt is incurred."

Exodus 22:2–3

The repeated "ifs" remind us that human beings
don't automatically obey God. Every "if" repre-
sents a moment of freedom. The possibilities for
both disobedience and obedience are endless. No
moral action is a foregone conclusion, but must
be achieved.

Which of these possibilities is open to you?

PRAYER: Holy and merciful Lord, I am aware of
the immense hope and trust you invested in me
by giving me freedom. Give me also your wisdom
and your spirit so that I can choose rightly and
courageously, living in love to your glory. *Amen.*

"Little by Little"

READ Exodus 23

"Little by little I will drive them out from
   before you, until you have increased and
   possess the land."

Exodus 23:30

The new life is a difficult life: in addition to developing a moral life in the community, there is the hostility of the enemies to face and defeat. None of this is going to take place overnight, but "little by little." It is the work not of a weekend but of a lifetime.

Are you prepared for the long haul in your faith pilgrimage?

PRAYER: Why am I so attracted to instant formulas, Lord? Everywhere in your scripture, and again here, you prepare me for a life of patient endurance. Keep me faithful as I renew my commitment to a lifelong obedience. *Amen.*

"We Will Be Obedient"

READ Exodus 24:1–8

Then he took the book of the covenant,
and read it in the hearing of the people;
and they said, "All that the LORD has
spoken we will do, and we will be
obedient."

Exodus 24:7

God has spoken; the people have heard. God has proclaimed his will to the people; the people have assented to that will. The covenant ritual—splashing altar and people with blood—gives a vivid picture of the essential life that occurs as God speaks in salvation and we speak in answer in faith.

How do you picture obedience?

PRAYER: It is so easy, O God, for words to be "just words." I lose connection with your living voice, and study your words instead of answering them. Give me ears to hear what you speak, and lips to confess my obedience daily. *Amen.*

SEPTEMBER 6

"The Tablets of Stone"

READ Exodus 24:9–18

The LORD said to Moses, "Come up to me
on the mountain, and wait there; and
I will give you the tablets of stone, with
the law and the commandment, which
I have written for their instruction."

Exodus 24:12

Leadership in Israel is not going to proceed by
force of personality but by the word of God.
So that that word will not be adulterated or modi-
fied by its interpreters, it is to be written—in
stone! Leaders are always subordinated to the
word of God.

Do leaders ever get between you and God's
word?

PRAYER: I praise you, God, for your word, written
and copied, preached and taught. I thank you for
all your servants who have faithfully brought it to
me so that I myself can listen to your word that
creates and saves. *Amen.*

"Take for Me an Offering"

READ Exodus 25:1–7

"Tell the Israelites to take for me an
offering; from all whose hearts prompt
them to give you shall receive the
offering for me."

Exodus 25:2

God wills to use what we willingly bring to him.
What we have and offer up, uncoerced, to him is
the raw material that he uses to work his will. Spiritual realities are made out of material offerings.

How many items are mentioned?

PRAYER: Almighty God, maker of heaven and
earth, help me to see that everything I have is material to be used in salvation. And make my heart
willing and generous to offer it for your use,
holding back nothing, in the name of Jesus who
gave himself for me. Amen.

"Make Me a Sanctuary"

READ Exodus 25:8–9

"And have them make me a sanctuary, so
  that I may dwell among them."

Exodus 25:8

The people are to have a place of worship: God is with them and they are never to forget. They are to make it according to exact instructions. The means of worship are important—it is not merely a matter of devout feelings and pious whims.

What does your place of worship look like?

PRAYER: How many times, God, people have heard you give similar instructions—build a place of worship! And how many times people have built them in devout obedience! I thank you for the place that I worship in and for the obedience that constructed it. *Amen.*

"Ark / Table / Lampstand"

READ Exodus 25:10–40

"They shall make. . . . you shall make. . . ."

Exodus 25:10, 17, 23, 31

The ark, table, and lampstand give a triple focus to worship: listening to the word of God (the ark), receiving the life of God (the table), and seeing by the light of God (the lampstand). Worship is defined by the Word, the Offering, and the Light of God.

What gives focus to God in your place of worship?

PRAYER: O Lord, I am so much more aware of my feelings in worship than of the God whom I worship. I thank you for every sign and representation of your life among us that keeps us attentive to you and detached from ourselves. *Amen.*

"Make the Tabernacle"

"Moreover you shall make the tabernacle
   with ten curtains of fine twisted linen,
   and blue, purple, and crimson yarns;
   you shall make them with cherubim
   skillfully worked into them."

Exodus 26:1

The most striking thing about this place of worship is that it is portable. What a contrast with the massive temples of Egypt! The tabernacle is the means to learn that we do not go to God to worship: God comes to us and accompanies us in our pilgrimage, each step of the way. We are never far from a place of worship.

What do you learn about worship from this?

PRAYER: Gracious and merciful Lord, I am forever putting distance between you and me; and you are forever coming to where I am, surprising me with your presence. By your grace I find that there is no place where I cannot worship. *Amen.*

"Make the Altar"

READ Exodus 27

"You shall make the altar of acacia wood,
   five cubits long and five cubits wide; the
   altar shall be square, and it shall be three
   cubits high."

Exodus 27:1

Worship is what we bring in offering to God. The altar and the court around it provide the means by which people can gather to bring themselves and their offerings. Because God is among us and gives himself to us, we come before him and give ourselves in response.

What in your church corresponds to this?

PRAYER: You call me to worship week by week, O God, and I assemble with my friends, your people. As we meet together in the place and at the time appointed, help us to be both *before* you and with each other so that we both receive your love and share it. *Amen.*

"Make Sacred Vestments"

READ Exodus 28

"You shall make sacred vestments for the
glorious adornment of your brother
Aaron."

Exodus 28:2

Certain uniforms define function. We see a person
dressed in a certain way and we know what to expect. The priest brings the people before God and
God before the people. The priestly garments
keep this function emphatically visible.

How does your clothing express something
important about you?

PRAYER: As I look at my leaders in worship and
discipleship, help me to see past the particulars of
their personalities to you, O Lord. I don't want
them to distract me from you but to help me
focus on you. *Amen.*

"Ordain Aaron and His Sons"

READ Exodus 29

". . . and you shall gird them with sashes
and tie headdresses on them; and the
priesthood shall be theirs by a perpetual
ordinance. You shall then ordain Aaron
and his sons."

Exodus 29:9

The priests are set apart for their holy work in an impressively elaborate ceremony. Praying is not casual work! Sacrifice is not a pious hobby! The most important thing in the community is what is taking place between God and his people; the ordination of the priests emphasizes the gravity and centrality of that work.

Who keeps you attentive to this central action?

PRAYER: I am grateful, Lord, to the people you have provided who proclaim your word to me, instruct me in the faith, and intercede for me in my weakness. Keep them faithful and strong in the work for which you have set them apart, in the name of Jesus, my high priest. Amen.

"Altar/Offering/Laver/Oil/Incense"

READ Exodus 30

"You shall make an altar on which to
offer incense; you shall make it of
acacia wood."

Exodus 30:1

Everything needed for worship has now been
provided for. We realize how much the senses are
involved in true worship. Worship leaves out
nothing; the act gathers our bodies, our money,
our memories, our needs—everything!—and lets
God integrate them in a life of salvation.

Is your worship adequately physical?

PRAYER: Father in heaven, help me to understand
Israel's experience in worship, what they did to
train me in a complete and unabridged presentation of myself before you as you do your work of
grace in my soul and body. *Amen.*

SEPTEMBER 15

"Bezalel"

READ Exodus 31

"See, I have called by name Bezalel son of
Uri son of Hur, of the tribe of Judah. . . ."

Exodus 31:2

Worship is Israel's chief work. The skilled artisan
Bezalel will make sure that there is nothing haphazard in the *means* for worship. The keeping of
sabbath ensures that there will always be adequate
time for worship.

Do you have both time and means for worship?

PRAYER: I live in a world, O God, that does not put
worship at the center, but way off on the edge of
things. But you put it at the center: transform my
perceptions so that I count coming before you in
praise and obedience as the chief work of my life.
Amen.

"An Image of a Calf"

READ Exodus 32:1–4

He took the gold from them, formed it in a
mold, and cast an image of a calf; and they
said, "These are your gods, O Israel, who
brought you up out of the land of Egypt!"

Exodus 32:4

The life of faith involves a lot of waiting, a lot of
not seeing. Impatiently and faithlessly we fashion
a substitute religion that reassures us with its accessible visibility, that caters to our wish for a god
who will show us what's next. The calf looked like
one of the gods that was popular in Egypt: now the
people were on familiar ground, now they were in
touch with reality. The demand for a faith that
works right now is subversive to a faith that waits
for God to reveal his will.

How do you express your impatience?

PRAYER: Lord God, you know how attractive this
"molten calf" religion is to me. It promises such
immediate results; it always seems so exactly
suited to my demands. I forget that it is made up
entirely of "rings of gold" and has nothing at all
to do with you. Protect me from its illusions in
the strong name of Jesus. Amen.

"And Rose up to Revel"

READ Exodus 32:5–6

They rose early the next day, and offered
  burnt offerings and brought sacrifices of
  well-being; and the people sat down to
  eat and drink, and rose up to revel.

Exodus 32:6

Religion as play is always popular. The gospel as
entertainment continues to draw the bored and
restless crowds. There is a genuine celebrative note
to be sounded in faith, but to use it to titillate and
divert is an outrageous sacrilege.

What are some instances of religion as entertainment today?

PRAYER: I look around me, Holy God, and find to
my dismay that the entertainment industry has
invaded the church. In the midst of the celebrity
glamour and frivolous antics, help me to keep my
concentration, in awe before the mountain of
revelation. *Amen.*

SEPTEMBER 18

"And the Lord Changed His Mind"
READ Exodus 32:7–14

And the LORD changed his mind about the
disaster that he planned to bring on his
people.

Exodus 32:14

There is a kind of foolish absurdity in Moses'
prayer. Who is he to oppose the cool logic of
judgment? Who does he think he is, arguing with
God? Still, here it is: Moses prays; God repents.
Grace eludes logic.

Have you ever been surprised in prayer?

PRAYER: Lord God Almighty, what an extraordinary privilege you have granted to me that I can
come to you in prayer. I don't have to acquiesce
stoically to fate; I can boldly ask you for mercy!
Keep me faithful in these prayers, in Jesus' name.
Amen.

"The Writing of God"

READ Exodus 32:15–20

The tablets were the work of God, and
the writing was the writing of God,
engraved upon the tablets.

Exodus 32:16

The stone tablets are in contrast to the golden calf.
The words in stone command what is highest in
us, a life of faith and obedience. The calf of gold
caters to what is lowest in us, making a religion of
animal appetites.

What other contrasts do you see between the
tablets and the calf?

PRAYER: Holy and eternal God, how grateful I am
for your word written. Protect me from all who
would divert me from listening to your word to
indulging in my feelings, who would seduce me
from obedient listening to pious fantasizing. *Amen.*

"Running Wild"

READ Exodus 32:21–29

When Moses saw that the people were
running wild (for Aaron had let them
run wild, to the derision of their
enemies), then Moses stood in the gate
of the camp and said, "Who is on the
LORD's side? Come to me!" And all the
sons of Levi gathered around him.

Exodus 32:25–26

The phrase is telling: "running wild." They ran
wild from God, from their commitment, from
the covenant. No inadvertent lapse, this was delib-
erate and violent rebellion. As a surgeon's scalpel
removes a malignancy from the body, the levitical
swords excised the rebellion.

What else do you know about Levites?

PRAYER: I live in a world that has such soft ideas of
sin, O God, that I am surprised at stories like this.
Does sin matter this much? Does it require such
drastic measures? I submit to your judgments; put
to death in me all that runs wild from your love.
Amen.

"Blot Me out of the Book"

READ Exodus 32:30–32

"But now, if you will only forgive their
   sin—but if not, blot me out of the book
   that you have written."

Exodus 32:32

Moments like these show us the immense stature of Moses. He is not a leader who uses the people to make himself look good or to feed his lust for power; he sacrifices himself to make the people good, quite willing to lose his life so that they can live.

Compare Moses' prayer to Jesus' going to the cross.

PRAYER: "Must Jesus bear the cross alone, and all the world go free? No, there's a cross for every one, and there's a cross for me" (Thomas Shepherd, "Must Jesus Bear the Cross Alone" in The Hymnbook, p. 290). Amen.

"But Now Go, Lead"

READ Exodus 32:33–35

"But now go, lead the people to the place
about which I have spoken to you; see, my
angel shall go in front of you. Nevertheless,
when the day comes for punishment, I
will punish them for their sin."

Exodus 32:34

Moses' offer is refused, but his leadership is
affirmed. The people must deal with the consequences of their own sin. Judgment, though,
does not put an end to their salvation travels; it
is what they experience while they travel in faith.
And they continue to have Moses' wise guidance
as they travel.

What do you think "punish them for their sin"
involves?

PRAYER: Lord God, this is more complicated than
I had thought: my sins get me neither total dis-
qualification nor a scot-free whitewash; I walk the
way of faith and experience the purging of judgment at the same time. Keep me steady and courageous in this pilgrim way, for Jesus' sake. Amen.

"A Stiff-Necked People"

READ Exodus 33:1–5

"Go up to a land flowing with milk and
 honey; but I will not go up among you,
 or I would consume you on the way, for
 you are a stiff-necked people."

Exodus 33:3

This is a dark moment: God withdraws his presence from the people. But with this ominous word
there is the promise of God's guidance ("an angel
before you") and his help ("I will drive out . . .").
There is a way out of the darkness.

Count the hopeful elements in these verses.

PRAYER: Do you never give up on us, God? After
all these centuries of our stiff-necked disobedience, do you still give hope and lead us on? When
I look at my sin I despair; then I look at the cross
of Jesus and take hope. *Amen.*

"Tent of Meeting"

READ Exodus 33:6–11

Now Moses used to take the tent and pitch
    it outside the camp, far off from the
    camp; he called it the tent of meeting.
And everyone who sought the LORD
    would go out to the tent of meeting,
    which was outside the camp.

Exodus 33:7

How can God wean the people from their Egyptian habits of religion as power, religion as fashion, religion as entertainment? How can he convince them that he is interested above all in personal relationship? He gives them a daily demonstration in Moses of what he wills for all, a meeting "face to face."

How does this shape your concept of prayer?

PRAYER: I come to this place and time for meeting you, Lord, with so much to learn, so much to unlearn! I have many wrong ideas of you, many false images. I return to these scriptures showing you in personal relationship as my Lord and Savior. Like Moses I want to enter the tent of meeting each day and have you speak to me as you speak to a friend. *Amen.*

"Consider Too"

READ Exodus 33:12–16

"Now if I have found favor in your sight,
show me your ways, so that I may know
you and find favor in your sight. Consider
too that this nation is your people."

Exodus 33:13

Moses at prayer—listening and asking; promising
and questioning; reminding and arguing. Moses is
bold and generous in prayer. It begins with his extraordinary "face-to-face" relationship with God,
but it goes on to insist on the inclusion of all the
people.

Does your life of prayer get beyond your private
concerns?

PRAYER: In the clamor of my own needs, Eternal
Father, I forget the needs of others. In the security
that I get from you, I forget the anxiety of others.
Make me as aware of the needs of others as I am of
my own, and keep me faithful in intercession for
them. *Amen.*

"In a Cleft of the Rock"

READ Exodus 33:17–23

". . . and while my glory passes by I will
put you in a cleft of the rock, and I will
cover you with my hand until I have
passed by. . . ."

Exodus 33:22

Moses wants to know God as well as God knows
Moses. Moses wants as much of God as he can get;
he gets as much as he is able to receive. The eager-
ness of Moses to know and the willingness of God
to reveal converge in the cleft of the rock.

How does God reveal himself to you?

PRAYER: "Rock of ages, cleft for me, Let me hide
myself in Thee; Let the water and the blood, From
Thy wounded side which flowed, Be of sin the
double cure, Cleanse me from its guilt and power"
(Augustus M. Toplady, "Rock of Ages, Cleft for
Me," in The Hymnbook, p. 271). Amen.

"Early in the Morning"

READ Exodus 34:1–4

So Moses cut two tablets of stone like the
    former ones; and he rose early in the
    morning and went up on Mount Sinai,
    as the LORD had commanded him,
    and took in his hand the two tablets
    of stone.

Exodus 34:4

The life of prayer that brought Moses face to face
with God (Exodus 33:7–23) brings the story to a
new beginning. That broken covenant and those
broken tablets are not the end of the story; with
the breaking of morning everything begins afresh
as God commands a new start.

What second chances has God given you?

PRAYER: "Morning has broken Like the first morning, Blackbird has spoken Like the first bird. Praise
for the singing! Praise for the morning! Praise for
them, springing Fresh from the Word!" (Eleanor
Farjeon, "Morning Has Broken," in The Hymnbook,
p. 464). Amen.

"Slow to Anger"

READ Exodus 34:5–9

The LORD passed before him, and proclaimed,
  "The LORD, the LORD,
  a God merciful and gracious,
  slow to anger,
  and abounding in steadfast love and
    faithfulness. . . ."

Exodus 34:6

God is not irritable. God does not have a short fuse. God is not on edge, ready to lash out at our folly and sin. Anger, yes: a passionate rejection of anything less than salvation for us; but conveyed in an incredible patience, in an endless (it seems) mercy.

How are anger and love related?

PRAYER: Frightened and guilty, O God, my impulse is to avoid you completely. Then I hear this "abounding in steadfast love" and realize that there is far more reason to hope than to despair, and I am back here, on my knees, pleading for pardon through Jesus Christ my Savior. *Amen.*

"I Hereby Make a Covenant"

READ Exodus 34:10–28

He said: "I hereby make a covenant. Before
all your people I will perform marvels,
such as have not been performed in all
the earth or in any nation; and all the
people among whom you live shall
see the work of the LORD; for it is an
awesome thing that I will do with you."

Exodus 34:10

The people are "tied in a living tether" (G. K.
Chesterton, "O God of Earth and Altar," in The
Hymnbook, p. 511) to God by command and ritual,
through worship and morals. No other covenants
are now possible. They have chosen, and they are
chosen—an exclusive relation.

What more does covenant mean in Jesus Christ?

PRAYER: Lord Jesus Christ, I want to understand
everything I do today as an aspect of the relationship that you have established with me, so that all
my thoughts and actions are in obedience to you,
and an offering to you. Amen.

"The Skin of His Face Shone"

READ Exodus 34:29–35

> Moses came down from Mount Sinai. As he
> came down from the mountain with the
> two tablets of the covenant in his hand,
> Moses did not know that the skin of his
> face shone because he had been talking
> with God.

Exodus 34:29

Moses' lengthy time with God was reflected in his face. But he did not flaunt his splendor—he veiled his extraordinary charisma from the people so that it would not distract them from listening to his message from God.

See how Paul uses this passage in 2 Corinthians 3:7–16.

PRAYER: Lord God, I remember the psalm sentence, "Look to him, and be radiant; so your faces shall never be ashamed" (Psalm 34:5) and realize that Moses did just that. I want to do the same, and experience in my praying the radiance of your glory throughout my life. *Amen.*

"All Who Are Skillful"

READ Exodus 35:1–19

"All who are skillful among you shall
    come and make all that the LORD has
    commanded: the tabernacle. . . ."

Exodus 35:10

Moses readies the people for the action of obedience. The commands have been spoken; the commands have been heard; now the commands
require action. There are to be no spectators to
this action. All are, in one way or another, to be
actors.

What obedient action will you engage in today?

PRAYER: How many times, Lord, have I walked
away from reading your scripture without a cor-
responding obedient action? I want to be a doer
of your word, not only a hearer of it. *Amen.*

OCTOBER 2

"Everyone Whose Heart Was Stirred"
READ Exodus 35:20–29

And they came, everyone whose heart was
   stirred, and everyone whose spirit was
   willing, and brought the LORD's offering
   to be used for the tent of meeting, and
   for all its service, and for the sacred
   vestments.

Exodus 35:21

An extraordinary willingness! There is no coercion, no forcing, no nagging. The word has gotten into their hearts (finally!), and an outpouring
of freewill offerings of material and abilities converge into making the place of worship.

What are you bringing in offering to God?

PRAYER: Stir my heart, Almighty God, as you
stirred the hearts of my worshiping ancestors. I
want everything that I have and everything that I
am offered up in worship so that you can make
something eternal of it. *Amen.*

"Knowledge in Every Kind of Craft"

READ Exodus 35:30–35

". . . he has filled him with divine spirit,
   with skill, intelligence, and knowledge
   in every kind of craft. . . ."

Exodus 35:31

Craftsmanship is not commonly listed in our "gifts of the Spirit." But here it is. The place of worship is made visually beautiful, and the ability to make the beautiful works is ascribed to the spirit of God. All who use their hands to the glory of God are hereby honored by Moses alongside prophets and priests.

Who do you know who uses manual skills in the service of worship?

PRAYER: I thank you, dear God, for all the men and women whom you have given skill to carve wood, weave fabric, shape metal, or cut stone, and who use their abilities to make beautiful sanctuaries for the worship of your holy name. *Amen.*

"Bezalel and Oholiab"

READ Exodus 36:1

"Bezalel and Oholiab and every skillful
   one to whom the LORD has given skill
   and understanding to know how to do
   any work in the construction of the
   sanctuary shall work in accordance with
   all that the LORD has commanded."

Exodus 36:1

Moses and Aaron, the prophet and the priest, are
unforgettable figures in the life of worship. But
why are not Bezalel and Oholiab also well known?
Words are holy—but so too are things. And the
people who fashion the things also work under
God's command to his glory.

Do you respond to beautiful things with the
same reverence as you receive gospel words?

PRAYER: I take so much for granted, God. You sur-
round me with evidence of a holy creation, and I
hardly bother to take a second look. Help me to
embrace all artists and artisans as companions in
the work of worship. *Amen.*

"More than Enough"

READ Exodus 36:2–7

". . . The people are bringing much more
than enough for doing the work that the
LORD has commanded us to do."

Exodus 36:5

This is one of the glorious high points in our history: a great generosity, a total commitment. And such a contrast to the grudging obedience and stingy support that often characterize religious groups. These worship breakthroughs occur when people hear and act on God's word among us.

Have you ever experienced anything like this?

PRAYER: "All things are Thine; no gift have we, Lord of all gifts, to offer Thee; And hence with grateful hearts today Thine own before Thy feet we lay" (John Greenleaf Whittier, "All Things Are Thine," in The Hymnbook, p. 555). Amen.

OCTOBER 9

"As the Lord Had Commanded"

READ *Exodus 39*

The Israelites had done all the work just as
the LORD had commanded Moses.

Exodus 39:42

Every detail completed. Every item made. All the
work finished. Much of the time our story is characterized by disobedience, failure, and rebellion.
But not always: obedience is possible; faithfulness
is an option. There are people who do what has
been commanded, and we can be among them.
   Are there times in your life like this?

PRAYER: I thank you, Lord God, for this record of
faithful obedience, so that I know this also as part
of my heritage: a people who not only hear the
word of God, but do it, pursuing excellence in
every detail. May this day's work by your grace
add to the accomplishment, through Jesus Christ.
Amen.

OCTOBER 6

"Made"

READ *Exodus 36:8–38*

All those with skill among the workers
   made the tabernacle with ten curtains;
   they were made of fine twisted linen,
   and blue, purple, and crimson yarns,
   with cherubim skillfully worked
   into them.

Exodus 36:8

In Exodus 26–31 the repeated phrase is "you shall
make." In chapters 35–40 the verb is "made." The
subject matter is the same; only the verb tense has
changed. Between what the people had been
commanded to do and what they did were their
great disobedience, Moses' great intercession, and
God's great forgiveness (chapters 32–34).
   What acts of obedience will you engage in
today?

PRAYER: Too much of my life is in the planning
stage, Lord. I want to get it into the building
stage—each day providing a record of what I have
done in fulfilling your command, in carrying out
your commission. *Amen.*

"Bezalel Made the Ark"

READ Exodus 37

Bezalel made the ark of acacia wood; it was
two and a half cubits long, a cubit and a
half wide, and a cubit and a half high.

Exodus 37:1

Bezalel needs to be more widely celebrated. He is
the one who got the commanded word of God into
visible, physical form. After the vision and the
preaching, there is the nuts-and-bolts obedience
in the craft and engineering of daily life.

Who do you know who is like Bezalel?

PRAYER: I love to hear and ponder your word,
Almighty God, but I get impatient in the actual
putting together of a life of obedience. There are
so many details! So many difficult angles! So
much intractable material to work with! Give me
the skill and patience of Bezalel so that I not only
embrace the life of faith but build it. *Amen.*

"Under the Direction of Ithamar"

READ Exodus 38

These are the records of the tabernacle,
the tabernacle of the covenant, which
were drawn up at the commandment of
Moses, the work of the Levites being
under the direction of Ithamar son of
the priest Aaron.

Exodus 38:

Another essential person, Ithamar: giving dir
tion, managing, organizing all the people in
multitude of tasks that add up to a comple
work. In the community of faith, management
administration are just as necessary as preac
and teaching.

Who do you know who is like Ithamar?

PRAYER: Lord God, as I realize the enormous
plexity of living the life of faith with all
people around me, each of us with differen
peraments and assigned to various tasks, I a
of appreciation for the Ithamars among u
guide and direct us in our work together
glory of God. *Amen.*

"Moses Set up the Tabernacle"

READ Exodus 40:1–33

Moses set up the tabernacle; he laid its
bases, and set up its frames, and put in
its poles, and raised up its pillars. . . .

Exodus 40:18

The purpose of these comprehensive instructions
for building the tabernacle and all the artifacts in
it is that the act of worship integrate and shape the
life of the people of faith in every detail. Worship
is not to be a matter of warm feelings and glow-
ing sunsets; it is a fact, physically there, forming
faith in them.

What force does the material place of worship
have in your life?

PRAYER: Holy God, keep me appreciative of how
physical, how material, all worship is. Remind me
that it does not rise and fall with my emotional
temperature but that it is an event commanded in
space and time. Amen.

"The Glory of the Lord Filled"

READ Exodus 40:34–35

Then the cloud covered the tent of meeting,
and the glory of the LORD filled the
tabernacle.

Exodus 40:34

We make the place of worship; God fills it. We
provide the visible structure; God provides the invisible content. Our obedience forms the place of
meeting; God's glory gives it meaning in grace
and mercy and salvation.

What does the word "glory" mean to you?

PRAYER: I get things so turned around, God. I think
that a church is successful when it is filled with a
good preacher (Moses!) and a lot of people. Now
I see that only when it is filled with your glory
does it mean anything at all. Fill my place of worship with the brightness of your presence. *Amen.*

"At Each Stage of Their Journey"

READ Exodus 40:36–38

For the cloud of the LORD was on the
tabernacle by day, and fire was in the
cloud by night, before the eyes of all the
house of Israel at each stage of their
journey.

Exodus 40:38

Worship is not what we do apart from our worka-
day lives; it is that which shapes and guides all our
comings and goings. Everything that Israel and we
as God's people say and do, day and night, is in
the context of the cloud and fire of worship.

Do you understand your whole life in the context of worship?

PRAYER: "Lord, come dwell within us, While on
earth we tarry, Make us Thy blest sanctuary, Grant
us now Thy presence, Unto us draw nearer, And
reveal Thyself still clearer. Where we are, Near or
far, Let us see Thy power, Every day and hour"
(Gerhard Tersteegen, "God Himself Is with Us,"
in The Hymnbook, p. 13). Amen.

OCTOBER 13

"An Offering"

READ Leviticus 1:1–2

"Speak to the people of Israel and say to
them: When any of you bring an
offering of livestock to the LORD, you
shall bring your offering from the herd
or from the flock."

Leviticus 1:2

None of us lives the way we should or as well as
we might before God who made and saves us.
None of us. Ever. The comprehensive term for this
perennial feature of human existence is "sin."
Leviticus provides detailed instructions for recog-
nizing and dealing with what has gone wrong.

Have you ever read Leviticus? What is your impression?

PRAYER: Dear God, as I embark on the reading and
praying of this third book of Moses, help me to
understand the realities behind these instructions
and learn to take both my sin and your forgiveness seriously. *Amen.*

OCTOBER 14

"A Burnt Offering"

READ Leviticus 1:3–17

"If the offering is a burnt offering from
the herd, you shall offer a male without
blemish; you shall bring it to the
entrance of the tent of meeting,
for acceptance in your behalf before
the LORD."

Leviticus 1:3

As we read these detailed instructions regarding
sacrifice for sin, one overwhelming realization we
get is that God does not treat our sins casually—
this is serious business! In the process, we learn
not to treat them casually either.

Note the important word "atonement" in verse
4. What does it mean?

PRAYER: It is hard for me to realize, Father, that
anything I do, whether good or bad, matters very
much to you. And yet, as I see what elaborate care
you took with my ancestors in regard to sin, it
must matter a great deal. Thank you for noticing
me, for caring for me. Amen.

"A Grain Offering"

READ Leviticus 2

> "When anyone presents a grain offering to
> the LORD, the offering shall be of choice
> flour; the worshiper shall pour oil on it,
> and put frankincense on it."
>
> Leviticus 2:1

The recipe for this offering is detailed and precise, as much so as for any meal. Moses trains us in taking as much care in dealing with the needs of the soul as with the needs of the body.

How many times do you find the phrase "pleasing odor"? Why do you think this is emphasized?

PRAYER: God, I very often find myself far more concerned with meeting my bodily needs than my soul needs. Give me both insight and determination to pay as much attention to the inside of my life as to the outside. *Amen.*

"A Sacrifice of Well-Being"

READ Leviticus 3

"If the offering is a sacrifice of well-being,
    if you offer an animal of the herd,
    whether male or female, you shall offer
    one without blemish before the LORD."

Leviticus 3:1

We develop quite a repertoire of sin (Hebrew has over two dozen words for it!). But God will not be outdone—he develops an even greater repertoire of forgiveness, as evidenced in this variety of sacrificial offerings.

In what ways have you sinned against well-being?

PRAYER: This sacrifice for well-being, Lord, reminds me of how essential peace is in your rule and salvation. And yet I am so frequently at cross-purposes with either you or one or another of your children. Forgive me, and give me your peace. *Amen.*

OCTOBER 17

"Sins Unintentionally"

READ Leviticus 4:1–6:7

The LORD spoke to Moses, saying, "Speak
to the people of Israel, saying: 'When
anyone sins unintentionally in any of
the LORD's commandments about things
not to be done, and does any one of
them. . .'"

Leviticus 4:1–2

Unintentional sin is no less sin than intentional
sin. Sin is sin whether we will it or not. None of
us has any idea of how much and how frequently
we sin. But there is no cause for either anxiety or
despair, because detailed provisions for forgiveness are already in place.

Do passages like this raise your "sin conscious-
ness"?

PRAYER: I live in a society, Lord, that brushes sin
under the rug, especially sin in the category of "I
didn't mean it." And here I find you dragging it all
out into the open, not to make me look bad and
blame me, but to clean me up. That's a surprise.
Thank you! Amen.

"This Is the Ritual . . ."

READ Leviticus 6:8–7:38

The LORD spoke to Moses, saying:
"Command Aaron and his sons, saying:
'This is the ritual of the burnt offering.'"

Leviticus 6:8–9a

The care with which the people bring their offerings to the Lord for atonement for sin is matched by an equivalent care by the priests who make the offerings. This step-by-step, detailed training in the handling of sin is, basically, training in forgiveness. The purpose of this seemingly endless attention to matters of sin is not to convince us of how terrible we are but to train us in receptivity to forgiveness.

Do you feel well trained in receiving forgiveness?

PRAYER: What a different emphasis this is, Father, from what I am used to—and how welcome! Instead of a blanket condemnation of sin, you offer a detailed exploration of forgiveness. You use my very sins as occasions to get close to me, to love me. What grace! *Amen.*

"Ordination Offering"

READ Leviticus 8

Then Moses took them from their hands
    and turned them into smoke on the altar
    with the burnt offering. This was an
    ordination offering for a pleasing odor,
    an offering by fire to the LORD.

Leviticus 8:28

It is no small thing to be designated priest—a person set apart to represent the people to God, to represent God to the people. The elaborate seven-day ritual, with its multiple sacrifices, marked both the complexity and the dignity of this essential work.

Have you ever attended a service of ordination? How does it compare to this one?

PRAYER: I thank you, dear God, for providing men and women for this work of priestly ministry—spiritual leaders who keep me on my toes before you, who keep your word fresh in my ears. Keep them holy and faithful in their work. *Amen.*

"Aaron Lifted His Hands . . . and Blessed Them"

READ Leviticus 9

> Aaron lifted his hands toward the people
> and blessed them; and he came down
> after sacrificing the sin offering, the
> burnt offering, and the offering of
> well-being.

Leviticus 9:22

The climax of the ordination was blessing. Everything a priest does is completed, finally, in blessing people. It is wonderful work and, when done well and obediently, is greeted with robust acclamation: "they shouted and fell on their faces" (v. 24)!

Who has blessed you most recently?

PRAYER: "Blessed be the God and Father of our Lord Jesus Christ, who has blessed us in Christ with every spiritual blessing in the heavenly places" (Ephesians 1:3). *Amen.*

"Unholy Fire Before the Lord"

READ Leviticus 10

Now Aaron's sons, Nadab and Abihu, each
took his censer, put fire in it, and laid
incense on it; and they offered unholy
fire before the LORD, such as he had not
commanded them.

Leviticus 10:1

There are details in this story that remain forever
enigmatic—we don't know enough of the context
to understand them. But the story itself is clear
enough: priestly work is holy work. It must not be
tampered with. It must never be used as a cover or
excuse for indulging oneself or exploiting others.

How many family members are named in this
chapter?

PRAYER: Dear God, I don't want to ever become
casual or calloused in regard to your holy word or
your holy work—words and work with which you
entrust me. Keep me alert and reverent always.
Amen.

"To Make a Distinction"

READ Leviticus 11

"This is the law pertaining to land animal and bird and every living creature that moves through the waters and every creature that swarms upon the earth, to make a distinction between the unclean and the clean, and between the living creature that may be eaten and the living creature that may not be eaten."

Leviticus 11:46–47

There is nothing more immediate to our survival than the meals we eat. To have an awareness of holiness worked into the decisions we make on what we will cook for supper prevents the holy from being confined to what takes place in worship and the sanctuary. Most Christians no longer consider these dietary restrictions binding, but our concern for a daily and earthy holiness continues.

Compare this with Acts 10.

PRAYER: Lord Jesus, you taught me to pray for my daily bread. Help me to be aware of your gifts and presence in everything I eat, discerning your holiness in my dailiness. *Amen.*

"The Days of Her Purification"

READ Leviticus 12

"When the days of her purification are
completed, whether for a son or for a
daughter, she shall bring to the priest
at the entrance of the tent of meeting
a lamb in its first year for a burnt
offering, and a pigeon or a turtledove
for a sin offering."

Leviticus 12:6

This passage is enshrined in Christian memory as
the occasion for presentation of Jesus in the temple by Mary and Joseph, the prayer and blessing of
Simeon, and the praise of Anna.

Read Luke 2:22–40 and compare the details.

PRAYER: I delight, Lord, in coming upon these long
and enduring continuities in my scriptures—the
bonds between ancient commandment and fresh
obedience that produce such song and praise. *Amen.*

"Diseases and Discharges"
READ Leviticus 13–14

The LORD spoke to Moses and Aaron,
 saying: "When a person has on the skin
 of his body a swelling or an eruption or
 a spot, and it turns into a leprous disease
 on the skin of his body, he shall be
 brought to Aaron the priest or to one
 of his sons the priests."

Leviticus 13:1–2

Our bodies are on equal footing with our souls
before God. As much attention is given to our
outward as to our inward condition. We inhabit a
tradition in which holiness permeates everything,
a tradition in which the healing of our bodies is
on a par with the forgiveness of our sins.

Recall some instances of Jesus dealing with
"diseases and discharges."

PRAYER: How glad I am, Father, that you care as
much about my body as you do about my soul—
and that Jesus has demonstrated that care in so
much detail, with so much compassion. *Amen.*

OCTOBER 25

"Separate from Their Uncleanness"
READ Leviticus 15

> Thus you shall keep the people of Israel
> separate from their uncleanness, so that
> they do not die in their uncleanness by
> defiling my tabernacle that is in their
> midst.
>
> Leviticus 15:31

Our culture pays as much, or more, attention to
these matters of sexual hygiene as did the Hebrews.
But for them there was more to it than bodily hygiene; there was also ritual purity. They sensed a
deep connection between sexuality and spirituality. We could do with a little more connection.

Do you see any spiritual significance to sexual
hygiene?

PRAYER: It always surprises me to find things I
have been taught were unmentionable in public,
out in plain view in the pages of the Bible. What
are you trying to teach me, Lord? That my life is
an open book to you? That nothing is left out or
unmentionable in getting my whole life right
with you? If that's it, I'm ready to be taught. *Amen.*

"Atonement"

READ Leviticus 16

"This shall be an everlasting statute for
   you, to make atonement for the people
   of Israel once in the year for all their
   sins." And Moses did as the LORD had
   commanded him.

Leviticus 16:34

This solemn annual act of worship centered attention on God's grace and forgiveness. Whatever
else God is, and there is much else, God is a for-
giving God. The atonement ritual gathered all the
experience of all the people into the merciful action of God.

   How many times does the word "atonement"
appear in this chapter?

PRAYER: Merciful God, how grateful I am for your
abundant and endless forgiveness. And what a gift
to have this ancient act of atonement reenacted
once and for all on the cross of Jesus! Amen.

"The Life . . . Is in the Blood"

READ Leviticus 17

"For the life of the flesh is in the blood; and
   I have given it to you for making atonement for your lives on the altar; for, as
   life, it is the blood that makes atonement."

Leviticus 17:11

Blood is both the material evidence and the symbol of life. As such, it became for the Hebrews a
constant reminder of what God gives and we must
not take away. In the sacrifices God used life to
give life.

What is the first thing you think of when you
see blood?

PRAYER: "There is a fountain filled with blood,
drawn from Emmanuel's veins; and sinners
plunged beneath that flood lose all their guilty
stains" (William Cowper, "There Is a Fountain
Filled with Blood," in The Hymnbook, p. 276). Amen.

"Do Not Defile Yourselves"

READ Leviticus 18

"Do not defile yourselves in any of these
ways, for by all these practices the
nations I am casting out before you
have defiled themselves."

Leviticus 18:24

Sexuality is our means to the intimacies of faithful
love. If it degenerates into exploitation ("uncover
the nakedness of . . ."), human lives are abused
and debased. One of the great gifts that Moses
brings us is high respect for the dignity and sanctity of our sexuality.

Who taught you sexual morality?

PRAYER: I thank you, God, for both the gift of
sexuality and the moral wisdom to develop and
practice it in sanctity and holiness. Give me the
intelligence and strength to follow your counsels.
Amen.

"You Shall Be Holy"

READ Leviticus 19–20

"Speak to all the congregation of the
people of Israel and say to them: 'You
shall be holy, for I the LORD your God
am holy.'"

Leviticus 19:2

These wide-ranging moral instructions touch
many, many aspects of life. Everything in life is
pulled into holiness—nothing is irrelevant. God
isn't interested in just getting fragments of our
behavior—he wants our total life in all its details
and parts.

Note the repetition of Leviticus 19:2 in 20:26.

PRAYER: Give me a discerning eye, Father, for all
the details and occasions for holiness. I don't want
to miss a thing; I want to live as well as you have
created me to live, holy the way you are holy.
Amen.

"I Sanctify Them"

READ Leviticus 21–22

"But he shall not come near the curtain
or approach the altar, because he has a
blemish, that he may not profane my
sanctuaries; for I am the LORD; I sanctify
them."

Leviticus 21:23

The priests, who are in charge of guiding the people in holy living, must also exercise care in their own lives. The detailed instructions train them to take their personal lives with the same seriousness that they bring to their priestly work. Holy work cannot cover up an unholy life.

What does the word "sanctify" mean to you?

PRAYER: God, I read these old instructions to the Hebrew priests and find myself wanting to be as careful about my life as you trained them to be about theirs. Help me to be always aware of your sanctifying presence in all that I do. *Amen.*

"My Appointed Festivals"

READ Leviticus 23

The LORD spoke to Moses, saying: "Speak
to the people of Israel and say to them:
'These are the appointed festivals of the
LORD that you shall proclaim as holy
convocations, my appointed festivals.'"

Leviticus 23:1–2

Regularly through the year, Israel gathered in
great commemorative acts of worship, remembering and celebrating the magnificent acts of God in
making and saving them. The calendar, in addition
to keeping track of time, kept track of salvation.

What "appointed festivals" have replaced the
ones named here?

PRAYER: Give me a good memory, Lord, a memory that is full of gratitude for all you have done.
Let the occasions of celebration and worship that
give shape to each year for me, recover all the details that make up salvation. *Amen.*

NOVEMBER 1

"Light and Bread"

READ Leviticus 24:1–9

The LORD spoke to Moses, saying:
  "Command the people of Israel to bring
  you pure oil of beaten olives for the
  lamp, that a light may be kept burning
  regularly. . . . You shall take choice flour,
  and bake twelve loaves of it; two-tenths
  of an ephah shall be in each loaf."

Leviticus 24:1–2,5

Worship is a place of illumination and nourishment. The light and the bread are always there, evidence of the character of the place, and of how our character is formed in such a place.

How did Jesus personalize this passage?

PRAYER: You, Jesus, proclaimed yourself "the light of the world" (John 8:12) and "the bread of life" (John 6:35). How fresh, how contemporaneous life now seems, with your words before me. *Amen.*

". . . Blasphemed the Name"

READ Leviticus 24:10–23

The Israelite woman's son blasphemed the
Name in a curse. And they brought him
to Moses. . . .

Leviticus 24:11a

Living in a culture where blasphemies like this
one are a dime a dozen, it is difficult to comprehend the seriousness with which Moses legislated
against blasphemy. Jesus was no less serious about
blasphemy, but he "improved" the legislation.

Read how Jesus used this passage in Matthew
5:33–37.

PRAYER: Lord, just because I have been introduced
to your incredible mercy, I pray that I may not
become casual about sin and its terrible consequences. Amen.

"Sabbatical and Jubilee"

READ Leviticus 25

". . . but in the seventh year there shall be a
   sabbath of complete rest for the land, a
   sabbath for the LORD: you shall not sow
   your field or prune your vineyard. . .
   And you shall hallow the fiftieth year
   and you shall proclaim liberty throughout the land to all its inhabitants. It shall
   be a jubilee for you. . . ."

Leviticus 25:4,10a

Sabbatical and jubilee years are provisions for social and economic justice. The ways in which we
deal with land and money and human rights are
as much a part of holiness as matters of sacrifice
and prayer and personal morality.

What are some ways that you see contemporary
American society being different in these matters?

PRAYER: Lord God, I want a large and encompass-
ing understanding of your will and your ways,
something that includes land and money and
other people—a *biblical* largeness and shape. *Amen.*

"Statutes and Ordinances and Laws"
READ Leviticus 26—27

"If you follow my statutes and keep my
   commandments and observe them
   faithfully, I will give you. . . ."

Leviticus 26:3–4a

What sometimes seems to outsiders like tedious
repetition in these chapters, to insiders is affec-
tionate rehearsal. For those who heard God's
personal word in these Sinai regulations and directions, it must have been a delight to hear it
again, to realize how much care God takes with
his children so that they get it right.

What has it been like for you to pray through
Leviticus?

PRAYER: God, I have a long way to go in learning
to pray. I tend to want my prayers fast-moving and
full of feeling. But the slow parts, I'm finding out,
have their own richness and beauty, and I
wouldn't miss that for anything. *Amen.*

"Take a Census"

READ Numbers 1–2

"Take a census of the whole congregation
of Israelites, in their clans, by ancestral
houses, according to the number of
names, every male individually. . . ."

Numbers 1:2

Organizing the Israelites was an enormous ad-
ministrative task, and absolutely necessary. They
already were a saved people and had become a
worshiping people. Now they were being prepared to be a missionary people capable of invad-
ing the promised land and taking possession of it.

Besides those designated for the census in
chapter 1, verse 2, how many more people do
you imagine might have been there?

PRAYER: But Lord, all Moses' counting and arranging isn't my idea of "spiritual" at all. Why not by-
pass all this with a strategically placed miracle or
two? Amen.

"Enroll the Levites"

READ Numbers 3–4

"Enroll the Levites by ancestral houses
and by clans. You shall enroll every male
from a month old and upward."

Numbers 3:15

Even while preparations for the mission were
under way, the Levites were singled out and set
aside to make sure that the place of worship and
the acts of worship were maintained at the very
center of Israel's life. Worship is the heart of the
life of God's people; the Levites were responsible
for making sure it stayed that way.

Who is responsible for maintaining the centrality of worship in your life and community?

PRAYER: Holy God, it is very easy for me to get
caught up in the hands-on work of mission and
slight the heart work of worship. But you have assigned "Levites" to me so that that won't happen.
Help me to listen carefully to them and to honor
their authority. Amen.

"The Lord Bless You and Keep You"

READ Numbers 5–6

"The LORD bless you and keep you;
the LORD make his face to shine upon you,
    and be gracious to you;
the LORD lift up his countenance upon
    you, and give you peace."

Numbers 6:24–26

As we go through page after page of these old instructions, designed to bring every detail of both sin and aspiration into the orbit of holiness, allowing ourselves to be impressed with the care that our ancestors gave to their lives, we are not infrequently surprised with blessings and realize that the same God who blessed them, blesses us—and so extravagantly!

How does a blessing like this (Numbers 6: 22–27) make you feel?

PRAYER: God of blessing, bless me. I want to receive all that you give, take it into myself, and then let it flow out into the lives of others, blessing them. *Amen.*

NOVEMBER 8

"Offerings"

READ Numbers 7

They brought their offerings before the
LORD. . . .

Numbers 7:3a

In contrast to our secularized world, which is obsessed with "gettings," the world of biblical spirituality is full of offerings. Offerings keep the arteries of faith clean and open, not sticky and clogged with things, so that grace can circulate freely, love course through our lives generously.

How many ways do you have of making offerings?

PRAYER: "Master, no offering Costly and sweet, May we, like Magdalene, Lay at Thy feet; Yet may love's incense rise, Sweeter than sacrifice, Dear Lord, to Thee, Dear Lord, to Thee" (Edwin P. Parker, "Master No Offering Costly and Sweet," in The Hymnbook, p. 299). Amen.

"The Levites as a Gift to Aaron"

READ Numbers 8

"Moreover, I have given the Levites as a gift
to Aaron and his sons from among the
Israelites, to do the service for the Israelites
at the tent of meeting, and to make atonement for the Israelites, in order that there
may be no plague among the Israelites for
coming too close to the sanctuary."

Numbers 8:19

Priestly work is not a one-person job. The work of
worship—bringing the people before God in repentance and faith and obedience, bringing God
before the people in revelation and promise and
holiness—is complex and arduous. And so Aaron
is given help.

What part do you have in assisting in the
priestly work of your community of faith?

PRAYER: I'd like to be part of this priestly work,
Lord. I'd like to accept some "levitical" task,
whether large or small, that can lighten the load
for my pastor. I want to participate in the wonderful work of bringing lives into your merciful
presence. Amen.

"Cloud by Day, Fire by Night"

READ Numbers 9

It was always so: the cloud covered it by
day and the appearance of fire by night.

Numbers 9:16

This experience permeates the Christian imagination: pilgrimage consists in waiting as much as in moving; God is in charge of the itinerary; the signs of his guiding presence are in the ordinary (cloud and fire), not the extraordinary.

How is your experience of God's guidance in your life given detail and affirmation in this story?

PRAYER: As I submit myself to your guidance, O God, help me to give up wanting to decide everything, insisting on being informed of the schedule, itching to always be "on the go." *Amen.*

"The Israelites Set out by Stages"

READ Numbers 10

Then the Israelites set out by stages from
the wilderness of Sinai, and the cloud
settled down in the wilderness of Paran.

Numbers 10:12

Spiritual pilgrimage is not occasional or make-shift, camping out by yourself or with a few friends. It is surrounded by an elaborate ceremonial that keeps everyone together, keeps the purpose ever prominent, and keeps worship (the ark) at the forefront always.

How does hurry interfere with your life of pilgrimage?

PRAYER: God, whenever I have a goal, I am more interested in getting there as quickly as I can on my own than in entering into the rich company of pilgrims and sharing a common life of obedience. Use these stories of Israel in pilgrimage to train me in the pilgrim life. *Amen.*

"I Am Not Able to Carry All This People Alone"
READ Numbers 11

> "I am not able to carry all this people
> alone, for they are too heavy for me."
>
> Numbers 11:14

No one, not even Moses, is capable of providing spiritual leadership alone. People don't become nice the minute they are saved—complaints and needs and questions pour in unceasingly, demanding attention. It's too much for any leader, even in a small congregation. But neither is any leader left alone. Elders are provided to share the leadership.

How do "elders" function in your church?

PRAYER: Thank you, wise God, for elders. Thank you for the men and women in my congregation who take leadership and share responsibility for building and nurturing community among us. Amen.

"The Cushite Woman"

READ Numbers 12

> While they were at Hazeroth, Miriam and
> Aaron spoke against Moses because of
> the Cushite woman whom he had
> married (for he had indeed married a
> Cushite woman). . . .

Numbers 12:1

Jealousy is poison in the spiritual life; and when it
occurs in leadership circles it is lethal poison.
God's quick intervention is antidote to the poison.
The leprosy on Miriam's skin was an eruption of
the jealousy within. But there is healing for both
leprosy and jealousy.

What experience do you have with jealousy?

PRAYER: Dear God, guard my heart from jealousy.
I want to cultivate a heart of intercession for those
with whom I work so that your word may be
freely expressed through them. Amen.

"Send Men to Spy out the Land"

READ Numbers 13

> The LORD said to Moses, "Send men to
> spy out the land of Canaan, which I am
> giving to the Israelites; from each of
> their ancestral tribes you shall send a
> man, every one a leader among them."
>
> Numbers 13:1–2

Here is our classic story of fear versus faith. Do we let fear reduce our lives to something timidly secure, or do we live boldly, expansively, obediently, and adventurously in faith? What words become decisive for our lives—the headlines from the newspapers or the witnesses of God's promise?

What "land" is before you right now to "spy out"?

PRAYER: I don't want to live on the basis of any "majority report," Lord. Help me to recognize the voices and reports of the Calebs and Joshuas around me, so that I can live boldly and obediently. *Amen.*

"Forty Years"

READ Numbers 14

> "And your children shall be shepherds in the
> wilderness for forty years, and shall suffer
> for your faithlessness, until the last of your
> dead bodies lies in the wilderness."
>
> Numbers 14:33

The history of our faith is full of this kind of
thing—complaints and rebellion and presump-
tion. And so "wilderness" is necessary to train us
in discerning reality, God's reality; necessary in
developing the character of obedience; necessary
to wean us from infantile demands and prepare
us to take on mature responsibilities—to grow
up "to the measure of the full stature of Christ"
(Ephesians 4:13).

Read Ephesians 4:1–16 for an account of spiritual maturity.

PRAYER: Lord Jesus Christ, I know that you have
promised to meet all my needs; but I often take
that to mean "all my wants" and throw tantrums
when I'm disappointed. Help me to grow up, to
learn and live the maturity that gives honor to
your name. *Amen.*

"A Blue Cord on the Fringe"

READ Numbers 15

The LORD said to Moses: "Speak to the
Israelites, and tell them to make fringes
on the corners of their garments
throughout their generations and to put
a blue cord on the fringe at each corner."

Numbers 15:38

Making the offerings and keeping the commandments is not an affair of grim duty—dogged and joyless. There is grace and beauty in it; "the blue cord on the fringe" is a wonderfully fitting reminder, not only of the fact of the commandments but also of the beauty in keeping them.

What touches of color and grace in your life remind you of God's commandments?

PRAYER: God Almighty, I am often stirred by the beauty in mountains and flowers, but I just as often overlook it in commandments and duties. Open my eyes to see the beauty not only in your creation but also in your commandments. *Amen.*

"The Affair of Korah"

READ Numbers 16

Those who died by the plague were
fourteen thousand seven hundred,
besides those who died in the affair
of Korah.

Numbers 16:49

Obedience is difficult. Rebellion is one of our most persistent sins. At some time or other we all want to have it our way, to be boss, to run the show. But sooner or later, if we are serious about being the people of God, we learn obedience.

Whose leadership do you have difficulty accepting?

PRAYER: Lord Jesus, you have placed people in my life to lead and guide me in your name. It is so easy to find fault with them, to second-guess them, and to foment discord because of them. Forgive my rebellions and train me in obedience. *Amen.*

"The Staff of Aaron"

And the LORD said to Moses, "Put back the
staff of Aaron before the covenant, to be
kept as a warning to rebels, so that you
may make an end of their complaints
against me, or else they will die."

Numbers 17:10

Aaron's staff, the sign of his priestly authority
among the people, was full of life, a flowering
and fruitful leadership. The leadership God or-
dains is not self-assertive, harsh, and coercive, but
light and blossoming. It is no less severe for all its
budding, but it is the God-graced vitality that
catches our eye.

What evidence of this kind of leadership do
you observe?

PRAYER: I have a difficult time holding these two
things together, Lord, the firm authority and the
vital grace. Continue to show me evidence of it
and train me in response to it, in the name of
Jesus. Amen.

NOVEMBER 19

"Responsibility"

READ Numbers 18–19

> The LORD said to Aaron: "You and your sons
> and your ancestral house with you shall
> bear responsibility for offenses connected
> with the sanctuary, while you and your
> sons alone shall bear responsibility for
> offenses connected with the priesthood."
>
> Numbers 18:1

"Responsibility" is the key word in this long stretch of instruction. Leaders and led in the community of faith are constantly *responding* to God's presence and command. All these carefully articulated instructions weave a network of responsible connections among God's people.

What specific responsibilities do you have in your faith community?

PRAYER: It is easy to take the stance of a consumer when I come to you, God: announce my needs and wait for you to fill the order. But this is a community I'm in; everything and everyone are interconnected. Show me my part in it and give me grace to live responsively and responsibly. *Amen.*

NOVEMBER 20

"Meribah"

READ Numbers 20

These are the waters of Meribah, where
the people of Israel quarreled with the
LORD, and by which he showed his
holiness.

Numbers 20:13

Two actual deaths, those of Miriam and Aaron,
frame this death-wish story: "Would that we had
died. . . !" (v. 3). But death and sin never have the
last, or even the central, word; God's abundant life
and holiness convert the people's life-denying con-
tentiousness into a continuing faith pilgrimage,
pushing death to the sidelines.

Read Psalm 95 as a commentary on this passage.

PRAYER: Gracious God, you do this all the time—
take my desires for the least, even for death, and
convert them into experiences of abundant life.
Thank you. *Amen.*

NOVEMBER 21

"A Serpent of Bronze"

READ Numbers 21

So Moses made a serpent of bronze, and
put it upon a pole; and whenever a
serpent bit someone, that person would
look at the serpent of bronze and live.

Numbers 21:9

There is a fundamental theme of spirituality in
this story that finds its full expression in the cross
of Jesus. The theme is this: God uses what we ini-
tially experience as punishment or disaster as, in
fact, salvation.

Read John 3:14–15 and John 12:32–33 and
compare them with this story.

PRAYER: My first impulse, Lord Jesus, is to run
from pain and misfortune. But you embraced it,
entered into it, and made salvation out of it. Give
me the courage to join you, and to experience the
fullness of a resurrection salvation. *Amen.*

"Balaam"

READ Numbers 22–24

He sent messengers to Balaam son of Beor
   at Pethor, which is on the Euphrates, in
   the land of Amaw, to summon him,
   saying, "A people has come out of Egypt;
   they have spread over the face of the
   earth, and they have settled next to me."

Numbers 22:5

This is one of the most extraordinary stories in our scriptures, full of humor, surprise, insight, and prophetic truth. It stretches our imaginations considerably to realize that God uses a pagan magus and a dumb donkey to accomplish his will.

Can you recall unexpected ways in which God has spoken to you or your friends?

PRAYER: God of grace and God of glory, help me to keep an open mind on the ways in which you speak and work, not boxing you in, not cutting myself off from the surprises of Spirit that you constantly bring into this world. *Amen.*

"The Baal of Peor"

READ Numbers 25

Thus Israel yoked itself to the Baal of Peor,
and the LORD's anger was kindled against
Israel.

Numbers 25:3

Zimri and Cozbi are not exactly household names
among us. We quite naturally shy away from
harsh stories like this. But when we realize that
this is not a story about a casual sexual indiscre-
tion, but that Zimri and Cozbi are political revolu-
tionaries attempting a bold coup, we are in a
better position to appreciate the zeal of Phinehas.
Their intent was to radically change Israel, throw-
ing out a holy God and substituting human desire.

What cultural practice today threatens the holiness of the gospel?

PRAYER: "Tie in a living tether The prince and
priest and thrall; Bind all our lives together, Smite
us and save us all; In ire and exultation Aflame
with faith, and free, Lift up a living nation, A
single sword to Thee" (G. K. Chesterton, "O God
of Earth and Altar," in *The Hymnbook*, p. 511). *Amen.*

"Take a Census"

READ Numbers 26

"Take a census of the whole congregation
of the Israelites, from twenty years old
and upward, by their ancestral houses,
everyone in Israel able to go to war."

Numbers 26:2

Numbers began with a census, a numbering of the pioneer people as they set out at Sinai for Canaan. With the exception of Moses, Eleazar, Caleb, and Joshua, those pioneers are all dead. Now, forty years later at the edge of Canaan, the census is repeated. It is an accounting that verifies in detail judgment on the parents and promise to the children.

Do you see any contrasts in how you experience the faith compared with your parents' generation?

PRAYER: Keep me ever mindful, Lord God, of how much I owe to my parents and other ancestors. Their experience of judgment in many ways prepared me for the experience of promise, and their history continues to be worked into my history; through Jesus Christ my Lord. *Amen.*

"Joshua"

READ Numbers 27

So the LORD said to Moses, "Take Joshua
son of Nun, a man in whom is the
spirit, and lay your hand upon him. . . ."

Numbers 27:18

Moses, instructed by God, commissions Joshua to
succeed him. It is a solemn moment, and holy.
These transitions are frequent and essential in the
leadership of God's people. No one person, not
even a Moses, is indispensable. No single style of
ministry is normative. Joshua's work would not
be possible without Moses. Moses' work would
not be complete without Joshua.

Have you ever experienced a transition similar
to this?

PRAYER: "God of the prophets! Bless the prophets'
sons; Elijah's mantle o'er Elisha cast; Each age its
solemn task may claim but once; Make each one
nobler, stronger than the last" (Denis Wortman,
"God of the Prophets!" in The Hymnbook, p. 520).
Amen.

"Offerings and Vows"

READ Numbers 28–30

The LORD spoke to Moses, saying: "Command
the Israelites, and say to them: 'My offering,
the food for my offerings by fire, my
pleasing odor, you shall take care to offer
to me at its appointed time.'. . . When a
man makes a vow to the LORD, or swears an
oath to bind himself by a pledge, he shall
not break his word; he shall do according
to all that proceeds out of his mouth."

Numbers 28:1–2, 30:2

More offerings and vows. Since they are not the
same offerings and vows we make, it is easy to
skim over the surface and pass on. What is useful
to realize here is the rich texture of obedience and
remembrance that results from a detailed obser-
vance of ritual and life. We want, by all and any
means in Christ, to reproduce that.

What are some of the ways in which obedience
and remembrance are ritualized in your faith?

PRAYER: When I realize, God, that faith, for my
Hebrew ancestors, was not ideas they talked about
but a way of life they lived, I am freshly eager to
find the particulars in my life that can give expression to my love for you. *Amen.*

"War Against Midian"

So Moses said to the people, "Arm some of
your number for the war, so that they
may go against Midian, to execute the
LORD's vengeance on Midian."

Numbers 31:3

This is Moses' last battle. Significantly, it is against
a people among whom he had lived in exile as a
shepherd and one of whom he had married (see
Exodus 3–4). But in the forty years since his exile
here, Midian had become an aggressive and seduc-
tive threat to the very existence of Israel (see
Numbers 24–25). The Midianites practice a religion that hates God and holiness. Midian is the
very antithesis of Israel. Midian has to go.

Do you think Augustine's phrase "a severe
mercy" is applicable to Moses' war against Midian?

PRAYER: Father in heaven, there is much here that
I don't understand. I don't understand "holy war."
But I do understand the danger of unholy religion. Help me to be vigilant against every attempt
to divert me from entering your holy land, embracing your holy promises. *Amen.*

"Be Sure Your Sin Will Find You out"

READ Numbers 32

"But if you do not do this, you have sinned
against the LORD; and be sure your sin
will find you out."

Numbers 32:23

Embedded in this old story, a phrase leaps out—it is still current among us! Morality does not change with the fashions. It is as persistent and unchanging as biology.

Which of the Ten Commandments seems to be most out of fashion in today's culture?

PRAYER: Dear God, don't let me ever get acclimated to the moral weather of the times. Keep me current with the old, eternal truths. Keep my moral sense as healthy as the circulation of my blood. *Amen.*

"These Are the Stages"

READ Numbers 33:1–49

These are the stages by which the Israelites
went out of the land of Egypt in military
formation under the leadership of Moses
and Aaron.

Numbers 33:1

It's time to review the forty-year pilgrimage. For
Christians and Jews it is the most influential and
fascinating travel account ever written. Our believing imaginations continue to be shaped by it;
our own sense of pilgrimage continues to be defined by it.

Recall three or four memorable camping places,
"stages," in your pilgrimage.

PRAYER: Eternal God, as I look back through the
years I realize how much more you were present
and active in the circumstances of my life than I
ever knew. As I remember and meditate, help me
to grow up and mature in your grace and holiness. Amen.

"In the Plains of Moab by the Jordan"

READ Numbers 33:50–36:13

In the plains of Moab by the Jordan at
Jericho, the LORD spoke to Moses. . . .

Numbers 33:50

Moses prepares the people for conquest and inheritance of the land promised to them. Nothing
is left to chance. Provision is made for bound-
aries, leadership, justice, and inheritance. Community falls apart quickly if these matters are
undefined or unresolved. The spiritual life is concerned with these as much as with prayer and
worship.

Do you divide your life into "spiritual" and
"unspiritual" categories? Or is it all integrated as
it was with the Israelites?

PRAYER: Lord, make me as at home accepting instructions in the plains of Moab as I am receiving
revelation from the heights of Sinai. I want to be
equally conversant with the spirituality of plains
and the spirituality of mountains. *Amen.*

"Moses Undertook to Expound This Law"

READ Deuteronomy 1–3

Beyond the Jordan in the land of Moab,
Moses undertook to expound this law. . . .

Deuteronomy 1:5

The people of Israel are poised at the entrance of Canaan, the land promised to them. Moses assembles the people and preaches this sermon, this document we call "Deuteronomy." It is a rehearsal of all they had experienced for the forty wilderness years, and an exhortation to assimilate the wilderness lessons and live God's promises.

Is this like any sermon you have ever heard?

PRAYER: Lord God, I forget quickly and easily. I need much and constant reminding. Use these Deuteronomy words to fix in my soul lessons learned, blessings received, and commandments given, so that I can live the totality of what you have prepared for me. *Amen.*

DECEMBER 2

"So That You May Live to Enter and Occupy"
READ Deuteronomy 4

"So now, Israel, give heed to the statutes
  and ordinances that I am teaching you to
  observe, so that you may live to enter
  and occupy the land that the LORD, the
  God of your ancestors, is giving you."

Deuteronomy 4:1

Moses preaches with the utmost urgency. This is
no dry rehearsal of history; it is passionately
preached history. The people are dealing with a
wonderfully alive and loving God, and they must
live at their faithful and obedient best in response.
The alternative is death. There is no in-between.

Are you conscious of living with strong and focused purpose?

PRAYER: The mood of my culture, God, is to live
journalistically, getting through one day after another, tearing off sheets of the calendar and dis-
carding them, letting the so-called news define
my history. But this sermon defines my history in
terms of your intents and purposes. This is the way
I want to live! Amen.

DECEMBER 3

"Two Stone Tablets"

READ Deuteronomy 5

"These words the LORD spoke with a loud
voice to your whole assembly at the
mountain, out of the fire, the cloud, and
the thick darkness, and he added no
more. He wrote them on two stone
tablets, and gave them to me."

Deuteronomy 5:22

The Ten Commandments are the solid, bedrock
foundation for developing a lifetime of authentic
human behavior, a moral life shaped by decision
in contrast to a haphazard life patched together
by whim and impulse. It is fitting that they are in-
scribed on stone.

Have you memorized the Ten Commandments?

PRAYER: Almighty God, inscribe these words also
on my heart. I like it that they were first on
stone—sure and dependable. But I want them
also deep in the tissues of my heart, shaping a life
of wise obedience out of my daily behavior. Amen.

"Hear, O Israel"

READ Deuteronomy 6

"You shall love the LORD your God with all
   your heart, and with all your soul, and
   with all your might."

Deuteronomy 6:5

If one sentence had to be selected to characterize
Israel's faith, this would have to be it. Israel's creed
is foundational to everything Christians believe
about God and to all the ways in which we respond to God.

   Notice the context in which Jesus quotes this in
Matthew 22:34—40. Can you find other incidents
in the New Testament that develop out of Deuteronomy 6?

PRAYER: Lord Jesus, keep this passage central to
my life. Don't let me ever digress or wander off
from this spacious and true center. Don't let me
ever be seduced into anything that would water
down my belief or distract my obedience. *Amen.*

DECEMBER 5

"Observe Diligently the Commandment"

READ Deuteronomy 7

"Therefore, observe diligently the
commandment—the statutes, and
the ordinances—that I am commanding
you today."

Deuteronomy 7:11

Obedience requires constant attentiveness. Multiple alternatives to "the Lord your God" are constantly set before us. Israel was trained to discriminate between the culture and the commandment. We need an equivalent training; without it we lose both our distinctiveness and our usefulness—our ability to be salt and light in the culture.

In what ways do you observe that culture is "a snare to you" (v. 16)?

PRAYER: Holy God, it is clear enough to me that you are working out your purposes for the world through my belief and behavior. I want to be of use to the world, not become like it. Help me to maintain my identity without becoming arrogant; help me to keep my distinctiveness without becoming aloof. *Amen.*

"When You Have Eaten Your Fill"

READ Deuteronomy 8

"When you have eaten your fill and have
built fine houses and live in them, and
when your herds and flocks have
multiplied, and your silver and gold is
multiplied, and all that you have is
multiplied, then do not exalt yourself,
forgetting the LORD your God, who
brought you out of the land of Egypt,
out of the house of slavery. . . ."

Deuteronomy 8:12–14

Extravagant blessings are accompanied by subtle
dangers. What is learned in adversity is often for-
gotten in prosperity. It happens all the time. But a
developed faith is as responsive to God when
things go well as when they seem to go badly.
Mature Christians are as practiced in praise as they
are in petition.

Does a full stomach dull your faith?

PRAYER: My praise reflexes, God, are not nearly as
quick as my petition reflexes. I yell for help the
moment I feel a need, but procrastinate my appre-
ciations. Tune my heart to praise your name!
Amen.

"Who Can Stand up to the Anakim?"

READ Deuteronomy 9–10

"Hear, O Israel! You are about to cross the Jordan today, to go in and dispossess nations larger and mightier than you, great cities, fortified to the heavens, a strong and tall people, the offspring of the Anakim, whom you know. You have heard it said of them, 'Who can stand up to the Anakim?'"

Deuteronomy 9:1–2

The life of faith is worked out against terrible odds—the Anakim! But faith does not calculate the odds; faith is a devout trust in God who does for us what we cannot do for ourselves. We never graduate from this life of basic trust. We can never be trusted to accomplish our own salvation.

How many instances of Israelite rebellion are referred to here?

PRAYER: How easy it is, Lord, to forget the sorry history of my stubborn rebellions, insisting on my own way, complaining about the conditions of your providence. And how easy it is, when blessings come, to suppose that they are a reward for good behavior. Keep me in touch with my need and your grace. Amen.

DECEMBER 8

"A Blessing and a Curse"

READ Deuteronomy 11

> "See, I am setting before you today a
> blessing and a curse: the blessing, if you
> obey the commandments of the LORD
> your God that I am commanding you
> today; and the curse, if you do not obey
> the commandments of the LORD your
> God. . . ."
>
> Deuteronomy 11:26–28a

Nothing in this life of faith is casual or unstudied.
The stakes are high. The issues are eternal. Obedience to God is never something to be taken for
granted. We need constant reminders to keep us
alert to both the breathtaking wonders and the
life-threatening perils.

How does Moses use the contrasting geogra-
phies of Egypt and Canaan to emphasize the new
reality in which the people are living?

PRAYER: I want to be as conscious of you, gracious
God, as I am of the weather, as responsive to your
commanding word as the earth is to the rain that
falls from heaven. You are the environment in
which I live; help me to be a good environmen-
talist. Amen.

DECEMBER 9

"The Place That the Lord Will Choose"
READ Deuteronomy 12

"But you shall seek the place that the LORD
your God will choose out of all your
tribes as his habitation to put his name
there. You shall go there. . . ."

Deuteronomy 12:5

Worship is not a matter of individual whim, of
doing something or other spiritual when and
where we feel like doing it. God assigns the conditions for worship. We worship truly not when
we have a "worship experience" but when we
respond to God's command and receive his
promise.

How many times does the phrase "the place the
Lord will choose" occur here?

PRAYER: I live immersed in a world of decadent and
disobedient worship, God—worship, so-called,
that is dictated by convenience and culture. I want
to worship you, Lord, not my own feelings. I
don't want to shape you into my image; I want to
be shaped into yours. Amen.

DECEMBER 10

"Treason Against the Lord"

READ Deuteronomy 13

"But those prophets or those who divine
by dreams shall be put to death for
having spoken treason against the LORD
your God—who brought you out of the
land of Egypt and redeemed you from
the house of slavery—to turn you from
the way in which the LORD your God
commanded you to walk. So you shall
purge the evil from your midst."

Deuteronomy 13:5

Monotheism, believing and worshiping the one revealed God, is under constant attack. The dangers we most have to fear are religious dangers—easy and attractive alternatives to the rigors and single-mindedness of obedient faith to the God who commands and saves.

What religious leaders ("prophets or those who divine by dreams") are you wary of in your situation?

PRAYER: It is difficult for me, Lord Jesus Christ, to maintain my focus on you and what you reveal to me of the Father. But I know I must. Give me a clear vision for truth and a faithful heart for love. Amen.

DECEMBER 11

"You Are Children of the Lord"

READ Deuteronomy 14–15

"You are children of the LORD your God.
You must not lacerate yourselves or
shave your forelocks for the dead. For
you are a people holy to the LORD your
God; it is you the LORD has chosen out
of all the peoples on earth to be his
people, his treasured possession."

Deuteronomy 14:1–2

God's relation to us is intimate and personal.
Awareness of this privileged status—"his treasured possession"!—is reinforced in dozens of ways in matters of daily diet and economics and justice. A sense of our identity as God's children comes as much, maybe more, from the everyday details of our lives as from the grand, divine purpose over our lives.

What are some details in your dailiness that contribute to your distinctive identity as God's child?

PRAYER: Dear Father, I know I am your child, chosen and blessed. But I often slip into being part of the crowd and lose a sharp awareness of who I am because of your love, of how blessed I am because of your grace. Help me to hear those words again, freshly and personally, "child of God"! Amen.

DECEMBER 12

"Three Times a Year"

READ Deuteronomy 16

> "Three times a year all your males shall
> appear before the LORD your God at the
> place that he will choose: at the festival
> of unleavened bread, at the festival of
> weeks, and at the festival of booths."

Deuteronomy 16:16a

The three major worship events each year for
Israel were designed to keep them *celebrative* before
God—not just putting one foot before the other,
grimly plodding through a daily obedience. There
are, of course, demands in the life of faith, but at the
center there is joy, an expansive and exuberant joy.

What keeps you celebrative before God?

PRAYER: In keeping track of all the little things I
have to do, O God, I often lose touch with the
large and eternal things that you do. As I worship
you, keep my perspective true, keep me living in
the joyful center of grace. *Amen.*

DECEMBER 13

"When You Have Come into the Land . . ."

READ Deuteronomy 17–18

"When you have come into the land that
the LORD your God is giving you, and
have taken possession of it and settled in
it, and you say, 'I will set a king over me,
like all the nations that are around me,'
you may indeed set over you a king
whom the LORD your God will choose."

Deuteronomy 17:14–15a

The details of preparing a holy people for a holy
life in the holy land seem endless. But they must
be made ready; these people must be prepared
and Moses prepared them. We can't help being
impressed by the patient attention that is given to
even obscure matters, the anticipation of the conditions in which they will live out the promise.

What leader has been especially useful in preparing you to live the promises of God?

PRAYER: "Jesus, lead the way Through our life's
long day, And with faithful footstep steady, We
will follow, ever ready. Guide us by Thy hand to the
Fatherland" (Nicolaus L. von Zinzendorf, "Jesus,
Lead the Way," in *The Hymnbook*, p. 334). *Amen.*

"You Shall Set Apart Three Cities"

READ Deuteronomy 19

". . . you shall set apart three cities in the
land that the LORD your God is giving
you to possess. You shall calculate the
distances and divide into three regions
the land that the LORD your God gives
you as a possession, so that any
homicide can flee to one of them."

Deuteronomy 19:2–3

The three cities of refuge, strategically placed throughout the land for accessibility, have come to symbolize in the Christian imagination the generous margins of mercy in God's justice. As we become acquainted with the history of our ancestors in the faith, it is refreshing to come across these innovations in mercy.

Are you as concerned with justice as with mercy? As concerned with mercy as with justice?

PRAYER: In my concern for justice, holy God, let not my heart become cruel. In my concern for mercy, gracious God, let not my heart become sentimental. Keep justice and mercy joined always in my life and my relation with others. *Amen.*

DECEMBER 15

"When You Go out to War"

READ Deuteronomy 20

"When you go out to war against your enemies, and see horses and chariots, an army larger than your own, you shall not be afraid of them; for the LORD your God is with you, who brought you up from the land of Egypt."

Deuteronomy 20:1

This is hardly what we expect in a tract on war: instead of emotionally rallying everyone to the cause, it introduces loopholes by which virtually anyone can be exempted. Even fruit-producing trees are exempted from being used for military purposes (v. 19). Even in war, maybe especially in war, life takes precedence over death.

Would you be an exemption if you had been addressed like this?

PRAYER: "Lord God of Hosts, whose purpose, never swerving, leads toward the day of Jesus Christ Thy Son, grant us to march among Thy faithful legions, armed with Thy courage, till the world is won" (Shepherd Knapp, "Lord God of Hosts, Whose Purpose, Never Swerving," in *The Hymnbook*, p. 288). *Amen.*

DECEMBER 16

"If . . ."

READ Deuteronomy 21–22

"If, in the land that the LORD your God is giving you to possess, a body is found lying in open country, and it is not known who struck the person down, then your elders and your judges shall come out to measure the distances to the towns that are near the body."

Deuteronomy 21:1–2

Community justice is worked out in complex conditions. "If" is the introductory word to much of Moses' counsel and guidance. It is not enough to have rules, we need detailed local knowledge of the social conditions in which they are worked out. Part of loving God, a strong theme in Deuteronomy, requires a wise and informed attention to human conditions.

Are you well informed on the living conditions in your community?

PRAYER: Almighty God, sometimes I want to nurture my faith on big ideas and glorious truths. Your word brings me back to deal with the conditions, some of them unpleasant, in which you are building a community of faith and justice. Help me to live faithfully and wisely in "the conditions." Amen.

DECEMBER 17

"Remember. . . . Do Not Forget"

READ Deuteronomy 23–25

"Remember what the LORD your God did to
Miriam on your journey out of Egypt."

Deuteronomy 24:9

More regulations. More direction. More counsel.
As the details pile up, we realize that God's commands to holiness and obedience and love are
never vague abstractions, but are always particular
items to be attended to in whatever communities
we find ourselves in. God's word is not poster cal-
ligraphy to decorate our lives; it is seed to be
planted in soil, the dirt of our lives.

Who keeps you responsible in daily round?

PRAYER: "So let our lips and lives express the holy
gospel we profess; so let our works and virtues
shine, to prove the doctrine all divine" (Isaac Watts,
"So Let Our Lips and Lives Express," in The Hymnbook, p. 289). Amen.

DECEMBER 18

"*Today . . . Your Agreement*"

READ Deuteronomy 26

"Today you have obtained the LORD's
   agreement: to be your God; and for you
   to walk in his ways, to keep his statutes,
   his commandments, and his ordinances,
   and to obey him."

Deuteronomy 26:17

The Lord agrees to be "your God" (v. 17); the
people agree to be "his treasured people" (v. 18).
There is no coercion here, no forcing. At the very
heart of the life of faith there is freedom: God
freely agreeing to be our God, we freely agreeing
to be his people.

Are you able to provide this kind of freedom to
those closest to you?

PRAYER: Thank you, God, for treating me with
dignity, for respecting my free will. Mostly what I
experience from others is manipulation and im-
position. Every time someone has a good idea or
a good cause, he or she seems to want to sign me
up "for my good," and I end up feeling crowded
and diminished. But not with you; thank you for
the great and spacious gift of freedom in Christ.
Amen.

"Ebal: All the Words of This Law Very Clearly"

READ Deuteronomy 27:1–10

"So when you have crossed over the
Jordan, you shall set up these stones,
about which I am commanding you
today, on Mount Ebal, and you shall
cover them with plaster. . . . You shall
write on the stones all the words of this
law very clearly."

Deuteronomy 27:4,8

Mount Ebal is roughly in the geographical center
of Canaan. God's word, written "very clearly" at
the conspicuous center of their new land, is intended to shape the Israelites' lives in every detail.
With a place of worship and a holy text at the center of their lives, the people have this constant and
unavoidable definition of who they are, "the people of the Lord your God."

Is there anything like a "Mount Ebal" in your life?

PRAYER: Glorious Father, you have set me down in
a world full of signs and reminders of your creative presence and your saving will. Keep me awake
to the signs, responsive to the reminders, so that I
will walk without stumbling or wandering in the
way of blessing. Amen.

DECEMBER 20

"Cursed Be Anyone Who . . ."
READ Deuteronomy 27:11–26

"'Cursed be anyone who makes an idol or
casts an image, anything abhorrent to
the LORD, the work of an artisan, and
sets it up in secret.' All the people shall
respond, saying, 'Amen!'"

Deuteronomy 27:15

We tend to associate cursing with bad manners,
or worse, evil conduct. But these curses are neither; they are clearly posted warnings against behavior that is deadly. They are the spiritual and
moral equivalent to the label "poison," or the sign
"hazardous waste." Familiarity with and respect for
the "curses" will give us a longer and better life.

What curses have you especially appreciated?

PRAYER: Lord God, thank you for the clear guidance, for not leaving me to find out everything by
trial and error, for protecting me from foolish or
ignorant actions. And now give me the grace to
listen to and affirm with my obedience the truth
of your revelation. *Amen.*

"Blessed Shall You Be . . ."

READ Deuteronomy 28:1–14

"Blessed shall you be in the city, and
blessed shall you be in the field."

Deuteronomy 28:3

There is a way to live that works, that prospers,
that is whole. Life—God-created, God-redeemed,
God-blessed life—is never trouble-free, but it can
be God-filled. The experience of blessing, the
overflow of God into our lives, is evident
throughout scripture and constantly confirmed in
faithful and obedient followers of God in Christ.

What blessings do you especially appreciate?

PRAYER: "Come Thou Fount of every blessing,
tune my heart to sing Thy grace; streams of
mercy, never ceasing, call for songs of loudest
praise. Teach me some melodious sonnet, sung by
flaming tongues above; praise the mount! I'm
fixed upon it, Mount of God's unchanging love!"
(Robert Robinson, "Come Thou Fount of Every
Blessing," in *The Hymnbook*, p. 379). *Amen.*

DECEMBER 22

"Disease, Panic, and Frustration"
READ Deuteronomy 28:15–68

"The LORD will send upon you disaster,
panic, and frustration in everything you
attempt to do, until you are destroyed
and perish quickly, on account of the
evil of your deeds, because you have
forsaken me."

Deuteronomy 28:20

This relentless exposition of the disaster that follows in the wake of disobedience is sobering reading. But it is also necessary reading. Our unaided and uninstructed imaginations are incapable of accounting for the moral, spiritual, and physical wreckage that results from a life lived in defiance of God.

What detail here appalls you the most?

PRAYER: It's hard for me to take all this in, Lord—the widespread social and personal and economic devastation that is caused by sin, my sin! Keep me mindful of the immense responsibilities that I have to live obediently before you for the sake of the welfare of my community and the health of my friends. *Amen.*

"It May Be . . ."

READ Deuteronomy 29

"It may be that there is among you a man or
woman, or a family or tribe, whose heart
is already turning away from the LORD our
God to serve the gods of those nations. It
may be that there is among you a root
sprouting poisonous and bitter growth."

Deuteronomy 29:18

At the center of this passage the little phrase "it may
be" is repeated twice. Everyone seems to be of one
mind on the plains of Moab, listening and responding to Moses, ready to enter the new land. But "it
may be" that there are some who are just going
through the motions, just going along with the
crowd. Moses probes them beneath the surface,
probes the hearts, not willing to lose a single soul.

Have you ever outwardly gone along with
God's people but in your heart held back?

PRAYER: I keep finding myself in this congregation, Lord God. Moses' preaching keeps searching
my heart, discovering my tendencies to hold
back, to secretly disobey, to privately withhold
faith. Use his preached words to make an honest,
strong, and courageous disciple of me. *Amen.*

DECEMBER 24

"The Lord Will Again Take Delight"

READ Deuteronomy 30:1–10

"For the LORD will again take delight in pros-
pering you, just as he delighted in prosper-
ing your ancestors, when you obey the LORD
your God by observing his commandments
and decrees that are written in this book of the
law, because you turn to the LORD your God
with all your heart and with all your soul."

Deuteronomy 30:9b–10

". . . *again* take delight" (v. 9). The Lord delights in
blessing his people. It is his most characteristic action. It is not occasional but repetitive. It is not the
exception but the rule. The warnings of possible
disaster, necessary as they are, are not the theme
of Moses' preaching. Delight is the heart of this
sermon.

Is your sense of God dominated by delight or
disaster?

PRAYER: "Sing praise to God who reigns above,
the God of all creation, the God of power, the God
of love, the God of our salvation; with healing
balm our souls he fills, and every faithless murmur stills: To God all praise and glory!" (Johann J.
Schultz, "Sing Praise to God Who Reigns Above,"
in The Hymnbook, p. 15). *Amen.*

"Not Too Hard for You"

READ Deuteronomy 30:11–20

"Surely, this commandment that I am
commanding you today is not too hard
for you, nor is it too far away."

Deuteronomy 30:11

Believing in God's word and obeying his commands are not complex, complicated tasks that
only a few especially talented and disciplined men
and women can carry off. This is not an elitist en-
terprise. It is not out of anyone's reach. It is not
beyond anyone's capacity. Anyone can do this.

Do you ever disqualify yourself from obeying
God's will on the grounds that it is too hard?

PRAYER: Blessed and merciful God, how grateful I
am to you for a gospel that is accessible, available,
and possible for even me. Forgive me for making
excuses, and give me grace continuously to confess with my mouth and believe in my heart that
Jesus is Lord and that you raised him from the
dead (Romans 10:9). *Amen.*

"You Are the One"

Then Moses summoned Joshua and said to
him in the sight of all Israel: "Be strong and
bold, for you are the one who will go with
this people into the land that the LORD has
sworn to their ancestors to give them; and
you will put them in possession of it. It is
the LORD who goes before you. He will be
with you; he will not fail you or forsake
you. Do not fear or be dismayed."

Deuteronomy 31:7–8

Moses led the people out of Egyptian slavery,
through forty years of wilderness trials, and right
to the brink of their new homeland. Now he steps
down and hands the leadership over to Joshua.
Joshua will lead the people into possession of
what God has promised. It's an impossible task
made possible by God's accompanying presence.

What impossible task has God made it possible
for you to do?

PRAYER: I'm ready, dear God, to do whatever you
set before me today. I'll not ask for more time, I'll
not claim incompetence. If you say I'm the one,
I'll be the one. Go with me, in Jesus' name. *Amen*.

DECEMBER 27

"The Lord Commissioned Joshua"
READ Deuteronomy 31:14–30

Then the LORD commissioned Joshua son
of Nun and said, "Be strong and bold,
for you shall bring the Israelites into
the land that I promised them; I will be
with you."

Deuteronomy 31:23

Moses and Joshua stand side by side before the
Lord, the one finishing his lifework, the other be-
ginning his. The two vocations are tongue-and-
grooved into the salvation purposes of God,
God-called, God-commissioned, God-used, and
God-blessed.

Whose lifework is closely linked with yours?

PRAYER: I thank you, O God, for fathers and mothers in the faith whose work makes my work possible. And I thank you, God, for brothers and
sisters who stand beside me in the faith, companions in obedience and love. Thank you for giving
my life purpose by calling me, and for making my
work possible by going with me. Amen.

"Moses Came and Recited All the Words of This Song"

READ Deuteronomy 32

Moses came and recited all the words of
this song in the hearing of the people,
he and Joshua son of Nun.

Deuteronomy 32:44

Moses has just preached a most passionate sermon; now he sings what he has preached in a
most eloquent song—the word of God, first said,
then sung. No matter how thoroughly and accurately the word of God is said, it is not complete
until it is sung.

What song of faith best expresses your faith?

PRAYER: "I sing the mighty power of God, That
made the mountains rise; That spread the flowing
seas abroad, And built the lofty skies. I sing the
Wisdom that ordained The sun to rule the day;
The moon shines full at His command, And all the
stars obey" (Isaac Watts, "I Sing the Mighty Power
of God," in The Hymnbook, p. 84). Amen.

"This Is the Blessing"

READ Deuteronomy 33

This is the blessing with which Moses, the
man of God, blessed the Israelites before
his death.

Deuteronomy 33:1

Deuteronomy is a pastor's sermon, Moses preaching the gospel to his congregation. He concludes
it with a twelve-part benediction, glorious blessings contoured to the needs and conditions of
each of Israel's twelve tribes. All the best sermons
end this way. Faithful preaching joined to prayer-
ful listening always results in blessing. Relish the
blessing!

Which of the twelve blessings best suits you?

PRAYER: "Blessed be the God and Father of our
Lord Jesus Christ, who has blessed us in Christ
with every spiritual blessing in the heavenly
places, just as he chose us in Christ before the
foundation of the world to be holy and blameless
before him in love" (Ephesians 1:3–4). Amen.

"Mount Nebo, to the Top of Pisgah"
READ Deuteronomy 34:1–9

Then Moses went up from the plains of
  Moab to Mount Nebo, to the top of
  Pisgah, which is opposite Jericho, and
  the LORD showed him the whole land.

Deuteronomy 34:1a

Moses' death did not provide us with a monu-
ment that we can visit. His death did not contribute to the business of religious tourism. Moses
provided a beginning, not an ending; his holy life
and visionary leadership continue still in the lives
of pilgrims like ourselves who live by God's
promises.

If you could choose your death, where and
when would you die?

PRAYER: A death like this, dear God, diminishes
my fear of death. When I see Moses' death completely encompassed by your providence, I realize
that nothing, not even my death, takes place outside your love and purpose. *Amen.*

DECEMBER 31

"Whom the Lord Knew Face to Face"

READ Deuteronomy 34:10–12

Never since has there arisen a prophet in
Israel like Moses, whom the LORD knew
face to face.

Deuteronomy 34:10

How fortunate we are to have Moses as our ancestor! His life and words provide such a massive and
firm foundation to our believing and behaving—
and all of it woven into a story that continuously
flows into and renews our God-authored stories,
these lives that we live to the glory of God.

How is your life different because of Moses?

PRAYER: Thank you, Savior God, for your servant
Moses. Thank you for calling him, for entrusting
him with leadership, for using him to provide for
your people, leading them to the brink of the land
of promise. Thank you for continuing to use him
to lead me in pilgrimage. In Jesus' name. *Amen.*

Topic Index

Scripture Index

12:4 Feb. 25
12:7 Feb. 26
12:10 Feb. 27
12:19 Feb. 28
13:1 March 1
13:8 March 2
13:15 March 3
14:2a March 4
14:24 March 5
15:5 March 6
15:8 March 7
15:18 March 8
16:2 March 9
16:6b March 10
16:10 March 11
17:5 March 12
17:17 March 13
17:26 March 14
18:2 March 15
18:12 March 16
18:20 March 17
18:32 March 18
19:14a March 19
19:16 March 20
19:29 March 21
20:2 March 22
20:17 March 23
21:2 March 24
21:10 March 25
21:17 March 26
21:22 March 27
22:1 March 28

22:8 March 29
22:9 March 30
22:13 March 31
22:17a April 1
22:23 April 2
23:2 April 3
23:17–18 April 4
24:7b April 5
24:12 April 6
24:31 April 7
24:50–51 April 8
24:58 April 9
24:64 April 10
25:8 April 11
25:12 April 12
25:21 April 13
25:28 April 14
25:34 April 15
26:1 April 16
26:7 April 17
26:18a April 18
26:26 April 19
27:4 April 20
27:27a April 21
27:36a April 22
27:41 April 23
28:2 April 24
28:12 April 25
29:11 April 26
29:16 April 27
29:31 April 28
30:22 April 29

6:25b July 1	15:1 Aug. 2
7:4 July 2	15:19 Aug. 3
7:12 July 3	15:23 Aug. 4
7:17 July 4	16:2 Aug. 5
8:6 July 5	16:7 Aug. 6
8:19 July 6	16:18 Aug. 7
8:24 July 7	16:22a Aug. 8
8:27 July 8	16:35 Aug. 9
9:4 July 9	17:7 Aug. 10
9:10 July 10	17:12 Aug. 11
9:24 July 11	18:1 Aug. 12
9:30 July 12	18:11 Aug. 13
10:11a July 13	18:14 Aug. 14
10:14 July 14	18:25a Aug. 15
10:21 July 15	19:6 Aug. 16
11:2 July 16	19:10 Aug. 17
11:5 July 17	19:19 Aug. 18
12:13 July 18	20:1 Aug. 19
12:15 July 19	20:2 Aug. 20
12:21 July 20	20:3 Aug. 21
12:31 July 21	20:4 Aug. 22
12:36 July 22	20:7 Aug. 23
12:39 July 23	20:8 Aug. 24
12:42 July 24	20:12 Aug. 25
12:49 July 25	20:13 Aug. 26
13:3 July 26	20:14 Aug. 27
13:14 July 27	20:15 Aug. 28
13:19 July 28	20:16 Aug. 29
14:9 July 29	20:17 Aug. 30
14:19 July 30	20:20 Aug. 31
14:21 July 31	20:24 Sept. 1
14:31 Aug. 1	21:1 Sept. 2